The Practical Guide to Higher Grade Poetry

by

David Cockburn

ISBN 0 7169 3149 4
© *D. Cockburn, 1990.*
(Revised 1997)

ROBERT GIBSON · Publisher
17 Fitzroy Place, Glasgow, G3 7SF, Scotland, U.K

CONTENTS

TO THE READER

This book is intended to do several things. It is first and foremost an introduction to poetry and poetic technique, especially for those readers who find poetry "a bit difficult". This book should help to make the subject that bit easier!

It begins simply and gently; it introduces you to basic poetic techniques — rhyme, rhythm, sound; and to the language itself. But then it changes direction, and introduces you to a kind of historical survey of poetry and poets. You will learn about Anglo-Saxon poetry, mediaeval poetry, Shakespearean poetry, Augustan poetry and Romantic poetry. It ends in the 1960s.

This book assumes no knowledge on your part of poetry or of the lives of poets. If some background knowledge is necessary or even (in the author's opinion) interesting, it is given. You'll learn about some ancient Greek myths, some Anglo-Saxon words, about Alexander III, and about how difficult it is to learn to spell.

If you are a candidate for Higher English, GCE A level, or you are studying English at University, you should find this book useful: it is intended to give you the background you may well have missed, to give you some history of the development of poetry, and to give you information about various pre-twentieth century poets. It is intended to make clear for you what is meant by "poetic technique". It is intended above all to be readable.

Poetry assumes greater importance in the Higher than previously simply because Reading assumes greater importance in the new Higher. You really do need to know something about the poets who were writing in the centuries before our own. You need to know something of the terminology of poetry. This book will give you all of that knowledge. It teaches you not only to be less frightened of Milton's poetry, or John Donne's, or Keats's or Browning's, but also how to enjoy their poetry. What people often don't realise is that pre-twentieth century poetry is much easier to understand than the poetry of this century because it is much less obscure. This book helps to make it even easier to appreciate.

The book is also intended for the general reader, the person who hasn't really looked at a poem since school. It puts everything into perspective without providing tedious notes, which always get in the way of enjoyment.

The book begins with the poetry of the cave-man and ends with Philip Larkin's sophisticated *Vers de Société*, written in the middle of the twentieth century — so it covers a vast time-scale in a short distance. But, as we pause at the end of the twentieth century, guessing and fearing what may well lie ahead in the twenty-first, the book allows us briefly to look back at our poets and see where we've come from. That in itself must be a worthwhile thing to do.

David Cockburn
Aberdeen, 1990.

– I –

INTRODUCTION

It's Thursday. You've had your tea — father is safely in the kitchen washing up, mother's in the hall starting a new DIY job, little brother is upstairs practising his first year French verbs, so you get peace to settle down to *Top of the Pops*. After all your favourite group is number one. You love the song, you listen to the words, you even sing along. You can't help it, because you love poetry.

Poetry? That's not poetry, that's my favourite group! Of course it's your favourite group, but they are singing a song, aren't they? And the song is just like a poem. But, you say, poetry is difficult to understand, you have to be good at English to appreciate it. That happens not be true; after all, the songwriter hasn't necessarily got an Honours degree in English Literature in order to write the lyrics. You certainly don't need an Honours degree to understand them. Your parents may well feel that they need some sort of degree to help them understand, but that's a different story.

– II –

POETIC TECHNIQUES

What is poetry, then? What is a poem? That question is actually very difficult to answer. Many people think that poetry has to do with rhymes, and although much poetry does rhyme, many modern poems do not. Rhyme, of course, can be very important to a poem. Read the following by Alexander Gray:

ON A CAT, AGEING

He blinks upon the hearth-rug	*a*
And yawns in deep content,	*b*
Accepting all the comforts	*c*
That Providence has sent.	*b*
Louder he purrs, and louder,	*d*
In one glad hymn of praise	*e*
For all the night's adventures,	*f*
For quiet, restful days.	*e*
Life will go on for ever,	*g*
With all that cat can wish:	*h*
Warmth and the glad procession	*i*
Of fish and milk and fish.	*h*
Only — the thought disturbs him —	*j*
He's noticed once or twice,	*k*
The times are somehow breeding	*l*
A nimbler race of mice.	*k*

ALEXANDER GRAY
(20*th Century*)

It is a very simple but amusing poem, and you can see fairly quickly that part of the humour is created by *rhyme*. What is rhyme? It has to do with words sounding the same — "cat" and "bat", for example. The rhyme certainly helps us to remember the order lines come in, but it also draws attention to words and can create special effects, some sad, some funny. The rhyme in the last verse of this poem helps create the joke — a joke which has been delayed until the last verse, but which is highlighted, pointed up by the rhyme.

Notice I have set out what is called a rhyme scheme — i.e. the pattern of rhyme throughout the poem. To establish the rhyme scheme, put the letter *a* after the last word in the first line — as I have done — and *b* after the last word in the second — if it doesn't rhyme. Whenever you come across a word which rhymes with the last word of any of the lines, then repeat the appropriate letter, and so on. The rhyme scheme in this poem is *a b c b* since the second and fourth lines rhyme in each verse. Now can you explain the joke at the end of the poem?

Another, perhaps more important, aspect of poetry is rhythm — the beat of the poem. A real craftsman can create some quite astonishing rhythms. Read the following poem carefully, then read it aloud once you've worked out what it is about.

FROM A RAILWAY CARRIAGE

Faster than fairies, faster than witches,	*a*
Bridges and houses, hedges and ditches;	*a*
And charging along like troops in a battle,	*b*
All through the meadows the horses and cattle:	*b*
All of the sights of the hill and the plain	*c*
Fly as thick as driving rain;	*c*
And ever again, in the wink of an eye,	*d*
Painted stations whistle by.	*d*
Here is a child who clambers and scrambles,	*e*
All by himself and gathering brambles;	*e*
Here is a tramp who stands and gazes;	*f*
And there is the green for stringing the daisies!	*f*
Here is a cart run away in the road	*g*
Lumping along with man and load;	*g*
And here is a mill and there is a river:	*h*
Each a glimpse and gone for ever!	*h*

R.L. Stevenson (1850 – 1894)

7

Clearly, Stevenson captures the noise, speed and rhythm of a steam train. He does this partly by repetition of sounds, words and by using rhyme, but mainly he repeats the sounds and words in such a way that you can hear the train chuffing at speed. Look at the first two lines and examine how he repeats the arrangement "Faster than fairies", and how the sound in "Bridges" is repeated in "ditches", "houses" is repeated in "hedges". These are not actually rhymes, but you can see how the repetition of the near-sound helps set up the rhythm. Another poem in which this is done to extraordinary effect is *Night Mail* by W.H. Auden — well worth searching it out to see how an artist can, in words, recreate the sound of an express steam train straining to climb the steep gradients of the Pennines.

Because I have started by talking about rhyme and rhythm, don't think that these two devices are therefore the most important. They are devices, as important as any other, but not any more so. Rhyme isn't essential to a poem and some quite memorable poems are rhymeless, as you will see later on in this book. Rhythm, however, is inescapable, though of course it isn't exclusive to poetry. Each of these sentences I am writing has its own rhythm and, as a conscious writer, I am aware of the rhythm as I compose. If the rhythm is monotonous and repetitious you, the reader, will become quickly very bored, but if I can vary the rhythm, sometimes fast, sometimes slow, sometimes using the rhythm to delay the main point I want to make to the end of the sentence for dramatic effect, then you won't drop off.

Rhythm exists whenever you use words, either as written English or, more obviously, as spoken English. Whenever you utter a sentence your voice rises and falls, you stress some bits of the sentence rather than others, you create a beat, rhythm. Some speech-makers — Hitler, Churchill, Martin Luther King — are able to exploit rhythm in order to hold or even manipulate their audiences. Just listen to a recording of Hitler's Nuremburg Rallies if you want to study how rhythm, timing, pace could so affect thousands of individual Germans that they lost their individuality and assumed unwittingly a corporate consciousness and identity. The mass of people began to think, feel and behave as one body. Rhythm in speech can be powerful. It can be used to create all kinds of effects.

It's the same with poetry. Or rather, similar. Poetry can have, though it needn't have, certain rules which impose the length of the poem, the

8

length of the verse, the length of the line, the rhythm itself.' The poet can choose to adopt a verse structure already laid down. So, before he writes his poem, the number of syllables or beats in a line is already determined by the poetic form he has chosen. Poetry written before the turn of the century tends to be like this — written to a set of rules. Sometimes the poet invented his own rules, but having invented them he then had to stick to them.

Look at this next poem, written by a contemporary of Shakespeare:

TO DAFFODILS

Fair Daffodils, we weep to see
   You haste away so soon;
As yet the early-rising sun
   Has not attain'd his noon.
      Stay, stay,
   Until the hasting day
      Has run
   But to the even-song;
And, having prayed together, we
   Will go with you along.

We have short time to stay, as you;
   We have as short a spring;
As quick a growth to meet decay,
   As you, or anything.
      We die
   As your hours do, and dry
      Away,
   Like to the summer's rain;
Or as the pearls of morning dew,
   Ne'er to be found again.

HERRICK (1591 – 1674)

Try working out the rhyme scheme for each verse. You'll see that verse 2 has exactly the same rhyme scheme as verse 1, but I am certain it will take you a little while to get it right. We do not at first notice that lines 1 and 3 are rhymed later on in lines 9 and 7. The complexly inter-woven rhyme scheme is: *a b c b d d c e a e* . Of course the rhyme contributes to the rhythm which is like that of a field of delicately swaying flowers, but the rhyme in itself reflects the inter-woven nature of the pattern created in the flowers by the breeze.

   The point is the poet has chosen a set of rules — the regular rhythm pattern and the complex rhyme scheme — which suit the kind of poem he wants to write. Once he has decided on the rules, he has to stick to them — they provide the framework for what he wants to say. His skill is in fitting word-choice and sentence structure into that chosen framework.

   Sometimes a poet chooses a very tight framework with even the number of lines determined for him. Wordsworth, in a poem called *Westminster Bridge*, has chosen the sonnet — a framework of fourteen lines with a definite rhyme scheme. Look at this poem carefully.

WESTMINSTER BRIDGE

Earth has not anything to show more fair:	*a*
Dull would he be of soul who could pass by	*b*
A sight so touching in its majesty:	*b*
This City now doth, like a garment, wear	*a*
The beauty of the morning: silent, bare,	*a*
Ships, towers, domes, theatres, and temples lie	*b*
Open unto the fields, and to the sky;	*b*
All bright and glittering in the smokeless air.	*a*
Never did the sun more beautifully steep	*c*
In his first splendour, valley, rock, or hill;	*d*
Ne'er saw I, never felt, a calm so deep!	*c*
The river glideth at his own sweet will:	*d*
Dear God! the very houses seem asleep;	*c*
And all that mighty heart is lying still!	*d*

WORDSWORTH (1770 – 1850)

   Examine the rhyme scheme: the *a b b a* rhyme scheme is repeated, then he has to repeat the *c d* scheme twice. Moreover, the rhymes have to be natural, as though they are an integral part of the poem, otherwise the poem will seem obvious and contrived because the rhymes are forced. Wordsworth achieves this natural feel because he is a good craftsman and can create a rhythm which is quite close to the rhythm of everyday speech. Read the sonnet aloud and you'll hear that it doesn't sound artificial and contrived. Some of the words may seem a little out-of-date — "doth" and "ne'er" — but the rhythm sounds modern. He succeeds in creating this "natural" rhythm by occasionally allowing a sentence to spill over on to the next line. For example, look at the second and third lines: "Dull would he be of soul who could pass by a sight so touching in its majesty". Now, although "Dull would he be of soul" sounds a touch poetic because the normal word order has been changed a little, nevertheless the two lines don't read as two lines of poetry; they could be two lines of prose. He uses the same technique further on in lines 6 – 7 and in lines 9 – 10. This device, where the sentence runs on into the next line, is called *enjambement* or *run-on line* and is quite commonly used by poets. We'll come across it later on in this book.

In this chapter I have looked at the question "What is a poem?" The question is almost impossible to answer, but at least in the attempt to answer it we have discovered some characteristics of poetry: it is written in lines; it always has rhythm, either regular or irregular; sometimes it rhymes; occasionally the sentence spills over on to the next line in a significant way and not accidentally as it does when we are writing prose. However, clearly there is more to poetry than these few ideas suggest.

– III –

SOUND

If silence is a characteristic of the novel, then sound is a characteristic of poetry. When you read a novel you enter silently and privately into the world created by the novelist: more accurately, perhaps, you re-create that world in your head, in your imagination. The point is that this experience takes place on your own in silence. Poetry may well have begun in the mists of time as primitive chants, or as part of very primitive religious rituals — long before Christianity evolved. By the year 1000 AD, maybe earlier, it had become an entertainment, recited most probably by court entertainers in a lively and dramatic way.

Originally, poetry was not a private experience and certainly not a silent one. The rhymes, which may have had magical significance, also acted as a mnemonic or aid to the memory, much as we use rhyme to help us remember the number of days in the months. A narrative poem of considerable length would be difficult to remember without rhymes to help recall it. Perhaps, in the millenium before television, the entertainment took place after a banquet or at the Court to while away the long hours before midnight. No doubt it would be a noisy and fairly ribald occasion; the audience, possibly intoxicated on pints of mead, could be inattentive at best, violent at worst. All the skills of the entertainer would be needed to capture its uncivilised attention. Along with the sheer power of the narrative of his story, the only other tools at his disposal were his ability to use sound to grip his audience and to control its mood.

Remember we are talking of an age that knew nothing of the printed word. There could be no written record of a story, no permanent means of passing it on from generation to generation. We are talking of a thousand years before the existence of the novel, when even a drama was fairly primitive in its construction and execution. There was only poetry: a narrative in verse form using rhyme as a means of its being memorised. But although there was only poetry for mass entertainment, it was popular. People listened to these tales of blood, thunder, murder and revenge. But the point is they *listened*: it was the sound that mattered.

In mediaeval times, the poem was still the main medium of entertainment, though the years had brought about a sophistication in poetic technique. By the second millenium, the long narrative sagas had given way to the ballad form, no doubt sung. The subject matter remained blood, violence, murder, intrigue, but there were also subtleties in the story. But they were *sung* — in other words, sound was still a hugely important component.

However, as I said, the ballad is altogether a more sophisticated form of poetry than had previously existed, and it used all kinds of techniques as well as sound. Much of the effect of the ballad depended on what was *not said*, but on what was implied. Let's look at the following ballad in more general terms.

EDWARD, EDWARD

"Why does your brand sae drap wi' bluid,
    Edward, Edward;
Why does your brand sae drap wi' bluid,
    Any why sae sad gang ye, O?"
"O I hae kill'd my hawk sae guid,   5
    Mither, mither;
O I hae kill'd my hawk sae guid,
    And I had nae mair but he, O."

"Your hawk's bluid was never sae red,
    Edward, Edward;   10
Your hawk's bluid was never sae red,
    My dear son, I tell thee, O."
"O I hae kill'd my red-roan steed,
    Mither, mither;
O I hae kill'd my red-roan steed,   15
    That erst was sae fair and free, O."

"Your steed was auld, and ye hae got mair,
    Edward, Edward;
Your steed was auld, and ye hae got mair;
    Some other dule ye dree, O."   20
"O I hae kill'd my father dear,
    Mither, mither;
O I hae kill'd my father dear,
    Alas, and wae is me, O!"

"And whatten penance will ye dree for that,   25
    Edward, Edward;
And whatten penance will ye dree for that,
    My dear son, now tell me, O?"
"I'll set my feet in yonder boat,
    Mither, mither;   30
I'll set my feet in yonder boat,
    And I'll fare over the sea, O."

"And what will ye do wi' your towers and your ha',
    Edward, Edward;
And what will ye do wi' your towers and your ha',   35
    That were sae fair to see, O?"
"I'll let them stand till they down fa',
    Mither, mither;
I'll let them stand till they down fa',
    For here never mair maun I be O."   40

"And what will ye leave to your bairns and your wife,
    Edward, Edward;
And what will ye leave to your bairns and your wife,
    When ye gang over the sea, O?
"The warld's room: let them beg through life;   45
    Mither, mither;
The warld's room: let them beg through life;
    For hame never mair will I see, O."

"And what will ye leave to your ain mither dear,
    Edward, Edward;   50
And what will ye leave to your ain mither dear,
    My dear son, now tell me, O?"
"The curse of hell frae me shall ye bear,
    Mither, mither;
The curse of hell frae me shall ye bear: 55
    Sic counsels ye gave to me, O!"

ANONYMOUS

brand: *sword*;   dule: *grief*;   dree: *suffer*.

    You will notice that there is much use of repetition in this ballad: the first line of each verse is repeated, and the fifth line is repeated; not only that, but the "Edward" of each second line, and the "Mither" of each sixth line is also repeated. There is only one rhyme in each verse — the fourth and last lines, and even then the "O" is repeated.

Nearly all poetry benefits from a second glance — all is seldom as it appears at the first reading. In this poem, after several close readings, we begin to build up a picture of the character of Edward and his mother. The last verse reveals much by implication: why does Edward curse his mother? The line is very surprising, and though the poem itself contains many shocking images, this perhaps is the most shocking because it startles us into a new awareness of the mother and of the relationship between the two of them. Has she driven him to the murder of his father? Look at her reaction when he tells her: "I hae killed my father dear": she seems unconcerned. In fact, she seems to be working up to the question: "And what will you leave your ain mither dear", to which he gives the shockingly disturbing reply which we have already noted. Although Edward commits the murder, it really is the mother whom we eventually end up despising. She seems insidiously brutal, callous, manipulative, and overbearing as far as her son is concerned; he seems able to escape from her domineering spirit only in the most violent and physical of ways.

Edward, Edward is an eighteenth century Scots ballad, really quite sophisticated and modern. As a matter of interest, here is one of the verses in the eighteenth century spelling:

> "Your haukis bluid was nevir sae reid,
>   Edward, Edward,
> Your haukis bluid was nevir sae reid,
>   My deir son I tell thee O."
> "O I hae killed my reid-roan steid,
>   Mither, mither,
> O I hae killed my reid-roan steid,
>   That erst was sae fair and frie O."

Spelling and rhyme are a guide to pronunciation, thus we know that "reid" must have been pronounced "reed" as it still is in the Aberdeenshire dialect, which we call the Doric. "Steid" is still pronounced "steed" in modern

English, and the spelling has changed to reflect the sound. Spelling, of course, in modern English is only a rough and sometimes unhelpful guide to pronunciation: thus, *rough*, *bough*, *though*, *through*, *hough*, *trough*. The other interesting word in the verse is "haukis". I shan't go into details of inflected languages and case endings — if you are really interested you can find information elsewhere, but "haukis" is the possessive, which we would nowadays spell as "hawk's" — reinforcing the point made in *The Practical Guide to Higher English* that the apostrophe is used to indicate that a letter is missing. English has long since dropped case endings, though they exist still in some pronouns — *I*, *me*, *my*, *mine*; *he*, *him*, *his*; *who*, *whom*, *whose*, and you'll notice in the possessive where there is a case ending, *my*, *mine*, *his*, *whose*, *her*, *its*, there is no need for an apostrophe because no letter is missing; in all other possessives you need the apostrophe to indicate a letter has been dropped.

Enough digression. The ballad is in that tradition of poetry where sound is of utmost importance. A ballad, as with all literature, is a comment on life and human values, but the ballad makes that comment by telling a story in a popular style. Ballads are invariably tragic, and the deaths in them reinforce the impermanence of life. They often involve magic, ghosts, fairies and witches which no doubt indicate that they belong to a tradition going back to the time before Christ. The following ballad chilled me when I first read it, and it still unnerves me a few decades on!

THE TWA CORBIES

As I was walking all alane,
I heard twa corbies making a mane:
The tane unto the tither say,
"Whar sall we gang and dine the day?"

"In behint yon auld fail dyke   5
I wot there lies a new-slain knight;
And naebody kens that he lies there
But his hawk, his hound, and his lady fair.

His hound is to the hunting gane,
His hawk to fetch the wild-fowl hame,   10
His lady's ta'en anither mate,
So we may mak our dinner sweet.

16

Ye'll sit on his white hause-bane,
And I'll pike out his bonny blue e'en;
Wi' ae lock o' his gowden hair   15
We'll theek our nest when it grows bare.

Mony a one for him maks mane,
But nane sall ken whar he is gane;
O'er his white banes, when they are bare,
The wind sall blaw for evermair".   20

ANONYMOUS

What is it about this ballad that is so chilling? There is something quite horrific about the difference between the tone of the two crows — they're having what is almost a cosy chat — and the sheer brutality and callousness of what they are saying.

> I'll pike out his bonny blue e'en

The description of his eyes as "bonny blue" hardly goes with the violence of "pike out".

But as I mentioned, it is what is hinted at that most appeals to our imagination. The description of or the portrayal of a violent scene is much less frightening (or violent) than a violent scene which is hinted at or suggested in an understated way. Our imagination has the power to create fear and violence far beyond the power of words or the television screen. It's no accident that Macbeth says "Present fears are less than horrible imaginings", nor is an accident that the most violent scene in that play takes place off-stage, the only blood seen by the audience being the blood staining Macbeth's and Lady Macbeth's hands. It's the same with this poem: it's what is not said, what is left to the imagination, that chills us. Who is the "I" in verse one?

> I wot there lies a new-slain knight

says one of the corbies. Now "wot" is the past tense of the Anglo-Saxon verb "witan" to know: we still use the word "wit" in the sense of knowledge — "he has his wits about him", "she is a lady of discerning wit". It's only recently that wit has been restricted in meaning to humour, funny or sense of humour.

However, back to the poem: why is the knight "new-slain"? Why does "naebody ken that he lies there" except his hawk, his hound and his lady fair? If he'd been out hunting, why was his lady fair with him — unusual in those days? We know that his lady has taken another mate — is that connected? What do you make of the last line— "The wind sall blaw for evermair" over the knight's white bones? It is so cleverly understated, the whole poem so economically written.

This next ballad, *Sir Patrick Spens*, recounts the tale of the death of the three year old Maid of Norway, who was drowned on the stormy voyage from Norway to Scotland.

In 1286, Alexander III had been thrown from his horse near Kinghorn in Fife and had been killed. This had caused a dynastic crisis since his only daughter, Margaret, Queen of Norway was already dead. The next in line to the throne of Scotland was the three year old daughter of the King of Norway. The ballad exercises a great deal of poetic and historical licence, and, in fact, since there are several versions of the ballad, it may well be a mixture of several stories.

SIR PATRICK SPENS

The king sits in Dunfermline toun.
   Drinking the blude-red wine;
"O whaur will I get a skeely skipper,
   To sail this ship o' mine?"

Then up and spake an eldern knight   5
   Sat at the king's right knee:
"Sir Patrick Spens is the best sailor
   That ever sail'd the sea."

The king has written a braid letter,
   And seal'd it wi' his hand,   10
And sent it to Sir Patrick Spens
   Was walking on the strand.

"To Noroway, to Noroway,
    To Noroway owre the faem;
The king's daughter o' Noroway,   15
    'Tis thou maun bring her hame."

The first word that Sir Patrick read,
    A lound laugh laughed he;
The neist word that Sir Patrick read,
    The tear blinded his e'e.   20

"O wha is this has done this deed,
    And tauld the king o' me,
To send us out at this time o' the year
    To sail upon the sea?

"Be it wind, be it weet, be it hail, be it sleet   25
    Our ship maun sail the faem;
The king's daughter o' Noroway
    'Tis we maun bring her hame."

They hoysed their sails on Monenday morn,
    Wi' a' the speed the may;   30
They hae landed in Noroway
    Upon a Wodensday.

                *   *   *

"Mak' ready, mak' ready, my merry men a',
    Our guid ship sails the morn."
"Now ever alack, my master dear,   35
    I fear a deidly storm.

"I saw the new moon late yestreen,
    Wi' the auld moon in her arm;
And if we gang to sea, master,
    I fear we'll come to harm".   40

They hadna sail'd a league, a league,
    A league but barely three,
When the lift grew dark, and the wind blew loud,
    And gurly grew the sea.

The ankers brak, and the tap-mast lap,   45
    It was sic a deidly storm;
And the waves cam owre the broken ship,
    Till a' her sides were torn.

"O whaur will I get a guid sailor
    Will tak' the helm in hand,   50
Till I gang up to the tall tap-mast
    To see if I can spy land?"

"O here am I, a sailor guid,
    To tak' the helm in hand,
Till ye gang up to the tall tap-mast —   55
    But I fear ye'll ne'er spy land."

He hadna gane a step, a step,
    A step but barely ane,
When a bolt flew out o' the guid ship's side,
    And the saut sea it cam' in.   60

"Gae fetch a wab o' the silken claith,
    Anither o' the twine,
And wap them into our guid ship's side.
    And let na the sea come in."

They fetched a wab o' the silken claith,   65
    Anither o' the twine,
And the wapp'd them into the guid ship's side,
    But aye the sea cam in.

O laith, laith were our guid Scots lords
    To weet their cork-heeled shoon,   70
But lang or a' the play was played,
    They wat their hats abune.

And mony was the feather-bed
    That fluttered on the faem,
And mony was the guid lord's son   75
    That never mair cam' hame.

O lang, lang may the ladies sit,
Wi' their fans into their hand,
Before they see Sir Patrick Spens
Come sailing to the strand.   80

And lang, lang may the maidens sit,
Wi' the gowd kaims in their hair,
A-waiting for their ain dear loves,
For them they'll see nae mair.

Half owre, half owre to Aberdour,   85
It's fifty fathom deep,
And there lies guid Sir Patrick Spens,
Wi' the Scots lords at his feet.

ANONYMOUS

skeely: *skilful.*
gurly: *surly, grim.*
wap: *stuff.*
or: *before.*

What, do you think, is the theme of this ballad? What point does it seem to be making? Look particularly at the last verse. There has been a build-up of atmosphere in this ballad and a careful suggestion of political intrigue. How has it been done? What devices and images are used to create the notion of a plot against Sir Patrick, and what techniques are used to suggest that a tragic end is inevitable? What of the Scots words? Are there any you find effective? It always strikes me that "gurly grew the sea" (line 44) is particularly effective: try translating "gurly" into English. You should also think about the importance of the story itself in terms of considering the effectiveness of this ballad.

– IV –

LANGUAGE AND POETRY

Poetry, then, until the 15th century, was largely an oral art form, which employed the devices of rhythm and rhyme to enable the performer to remember the story. But the 15th century brought with it an invention which was to have a dramatic and permanent effect on art, civilisation and culture. William Caxton, in 1476, returned to England having mastered the newly-developed art of printing. He set himself up in offices attached to Westminster Abbey and began to print pamphlets, books, and among other things the works of Geoffrey Chaucer. Until the 15th century, the only method of recording knowledge, poetry, stories, history was to use pen and ink. Many monks devoted their entire lives to the copying, sometimes in a highly ornate manner, of books and manuscripts. The very word *manuscript* means written by hand. Obviously, because of the effort and time involved, there could be very few copies of any one book. There could be only very few libraries and bookshops, and, of course, there could be very few people who were able to read and write: there was no need and certainly little opportunity to learn. The vast majority of people had no access to the written word.

Then came the printing press, and within a few short years mankind's memory had billions of bytes added to it. Now there could be a permanent record and the education of more than a tiny élite could begin. Once literate, people were no longer dependent on oral/aural entertainment, but could read stories for themselves. Poetry was no longer merely the spoken word, but could now have the permanence and accessibility of the printed page. Which of course meant that the line ending and the rhyme were no longer solely mnemonic devices, but could take on a significance available only to a reader. Though still it has to be stressed that thousands of years of the element of sound in poetry could not and still must not be ignored.

Let's go back in time a bit. From the time of Christ much happened to our native language: the invasion of Britain by the Romans, then by the Angles, Jutes and Saxons, and finally, in 1066, by the Normans. Each invasion in turn brought with it a new culture and a new language, both of which suffused and, at times, replaced the native culture and language. The process was very complex, but let's briefly look at the period before and just after the success of William the Conqueror in 1066. From about 600 AD to 1100 AD the language spoken in this country is known as Old English or Anglo-Saxon and is largely unrecognisable today, though some vocabulary items have remained more or less intact:

Aelc þāra þe þās mīn word ġe·hierþ
Each who these my words hears

his hūs ofer stān ġe·timbrode
his house over stones builds.

If I tell you the letter "þ" is pronounced "th", then you can see some similarities: "þās" for "these", "ġe·hierþ" for "hears" or "heareth". "Word" is still the same, and "hūs" is still "hoose" in modern Scots. "Stān" (the vowel is pronounced as in "flan") is the modern Scots word "stane".

But by 1100, the effects of the Norman invasion were beginning to be felt, and from then to 1400 is the period known as Middle English. French began to creep into the language of the educated classes, especially at court and in government (both French words). The country at large still spoke English, but French was the language of the educated élite. English gradually became accepted as the speech of the Upper Classes, and towards the end of the 14th century, Geoffrey Chaucer, an educated man attached to the Court, wrote his *Canterbury Tales* in English. Look at the first few lines of the Prologue to the *Canterbury Tales*:

Whan that *Aprill* with his shoures sote
The droghte of *March* hath *perced* to the rote,
And bathed every *veine* in swich *licour*
Of which *vertu engendred* is the *flour*,
Whan Zephirus eek with his swete breth
Inspired hath in every holt and heth
The *tendre* croppes, and the yonge sonne

23

Hate in the Ram his halve *cours* yronne,
And smale foules maken *melodye*
That slepen al the nyght with open ye,
Than longen folk to goon on *pilgrimages* . . .

The italicised words are French, but if you read the passage aloud you'll be surprised how much you can understand even although it's about 600 years old. For the words you don't recognise, here is a useful tip: leave the consonants as they are, play around with the vowels, and drop the final "e". Thus "swich" is "such" and "tendre" is "tender".

Chaucer died in 1400; his influence on the development of English is startling. He helped to establish, by making a written record, the grammar syntax and spelling of the language. One of the functions of poetry, if it can be said to have a function, is not just to record how the language is being used at the time of writing but is also to influence the very development of the language. The English that you and I speak and write today might well have been quite different had Chaucer never been born. From his death in 1400 until the end of the century, English moved into the period we now think of as Modern English. It took about 150 years from Chaucer's death before the language becomes recognisable to us today. But towards the end of the 16th century the vocabulary and structures are much more accessible to us, though the meaning may not be the same as ours. The major poets writing at this time are Sir Walter Raleigh and Edmund Spenser. The language of the following poem by Raleigh, I think you'll agree, is completely recognisable and comprehensible:

THE CONCLUSION

Even such is Time, that takes in trust
    Our youth, our joys, our all we have,
And pays us but with earth and dust;
Who in the dark and silent grave,
When we have wandered all our ways,
Shuts up the story of our days;
But from this earth, this grave, this dust,
My God shall raise me up, I trust.

24

Now with all poetry, even with Chaucer's poetry, you must go by and trust your own reactions. Don't read it then consult a book to find out what someone else thinks the poem is about. Trust your own reaction and your own judgement. The language of *The Conclusion* is recognisable, but what does that language say to you? Titles are always a help — Conclusion: conclusion of what? Life? Things conclude in the sense that they come to an end, but we also use the word "conclusion" in another sense: we come to a conclusion after having been puzzled about something. Can the word here be meant in both senses: the conclusion, the end, of life, and the conclusion about life that we come to as we end it? What is the poem, then, about: Time? The grave? And is that the end?

> But from this earth, this grave, this dust,
> My God shall raise me up, I trust.

So it's about life after death, as well. Look at the position of "I trust" — it rhymes, significantly, with "dust", and because it forms the last two words of the poem, takes on further significance. We use "I trust" casually to mean "I hope", but Raleigh makes clear here that "I trust" is meant in the sense of trusting someone — in this case God and His pledge to give us everlasting life.

– V –

SIXTEENTH AND SEVENTEENTH CENTURIES

SHAKESPEARE

In the 52 years from 1564 to 1616, there lived a man whose contribution to English is still unsurpassed. The language he used, the ideas he expressed and the images he created are still current in the consciousness of us all today. His influence on subsequent writers and thinkers has been immeasurable. He must rank among the greatest geniuses of all time. His name is William Shakespeare. Although he is best known for certain of his plays, he wrote 37 in all, his output of poetry was voluminous.

The poetry we have looked at so far has had the hallmarks of rhythm and rhyme, but Shakespeare brought to poetry — especially the poetry in his dramas — blank verse: that is, poetry which does not rhyme. Not that he invented blank verse, but his technical mastery of it, combined with his imaginative genius, creates for us a blank verse that is both startling and memorable.

Let's examine some lines from Act V of *Macbeth*. Macbeth has just been informed of his wife's death —

Seyton: The Queen, my lord, is dead.

Macbeth: She should have died hereafter;
          There would have been a time for such a word.
          Tomorrow and tomorrow and tomorrow,
          Creeps in this petty pace from day to day
          To the last syllable of recorded time,
          And all our yesterdays have lighted fools
          The way to dusty death. Out, out, brief candle!
          Life's but a walking shadow, a poor player
          That struts and frets his hour upon the stage
          And then is heard no more: it is a tale
          Told by an idiot, full of sound and fury,
          Signifying nothing.

26

Now right away you can see that this twelve line piece of poetry does not rhyme. But let's examine in detail the rhythm. Take the second line of Macbeth's speech:

⏑ ´ ⏑ ´ ⏑´ ⏑ ´ ⏑´
There would have been a time for such a word.

The ⏑ indicates a weak stress and the ´ indicates a strong one. So the pattern is *weak strong, weak strong, weak strong, weak strong, weak strong*. Which is remarkably similar to the stress pattern of everyday speech. If we count each *weak strong* as one unit or *foot* as it's technically called, then you'll see that there are five feet. Take the fourth line:

⏑ ´⏑ ´⏑ ´ ⏑ ´⏑ ´
Creeps in this petty pace from day to day

Again there are five feet. In fact nearly all the lines have five feet. But look at the third line:

⏑ ´ ⏑´ ⏑ ´ ⏑ ´ ⏑ ´ ⏑
Tomorrow and tomorrow and tomorrow

Note that the "and" gets a strong stress, which is unusual — conjunctions aren't normally very important words, not to the extent of giving them a strong stress anyway — but count the feet. There are five with a weak stress left over. This deliberately draws attention to the line because the natural rhythm has been broken, but it also draws attention to the word "tomorrow". Shakespeare does more than merely use the technical device of repetition. See what I mean about his technical expertise?

Once you note the "tomorrow" — word of time — you then note the ending of the next line:

⏑ ´
to day

which is exactly how we pronounce "today" — another time word. Two lines on and Macbeth talks about "all our yesterdays" — the only other time word left. Tomorrow, today, yesterday: Macbeth is obsessed with time. Now look back at the first line of his speech: "She should have died hereafter".

27

"Hereafter" is yet another time word, but it also refers to that non-temporal existence after death. His obsession then is with time and death. Some people think that the line "She should have died hereafter" indicates Macbeth's annoyance with Lady Macbeth's inconsiderate timing; that he dismisses her death as a bit of a nuisance right now, considering all the other bits and pieces on his mind. But I think that's too glib an explanation: "hereafter" does not mean "some other time", but is an indication of Macbeth's intensely depressed state of mind. He is now glimpsing the pointlessness, the emptiness, the folly and the brevity of existence. By "all our yesterdays" he means (among other things) man's collective experience — and what does that do for us? It merely lights fools the way to dusty death. Look at the connotative area of "dusty" which includes the allusion "Ashes to ashes, dust to dust". "Candle" is often used as a symbol of life, but Macbeth calls it brief.

Then he switches the metaphor to the stage, used often by Shakespeare as a symbol of the world. Macbeth says that our life is like that of a "walking shadow" — "walking shadow" was the name given to an actor with a walk-on part, again a reference to the brevity of existence. The actor "struts and frets" his "hour" upon the stage, after which moment of inglory he is "heard no more", all of which refer to the pain and pointlessness of existence. These images are intensified by "a tale/told by an idiot" and then the utter hollowness and emptiness of "nothing".

Remember what I said in Chapter II about end-stop lines and run-on lines? All right then, you work out how they are used in Macbeth's speech and why. The sentence structure doesn't quite fit the verse structure which means an actor delivering the lines has to use all his skill in delivering the line while retaining the syntax of the sentences. A bad actor will concentrate on line endings to the extent that meaning is fractured, while a mediocre one will deliver the sentences while ignoring the rhythm and the poetry.

The above analysis of the twelve lines from *Macbeth* may teach you quite a bit about the technical devices in poetry, but there is another more general lesson to be learned: a poem gives up its meaning gradually the more you read and study it. It is unlikely, if not impossible, to get everything there is out of a poem at the first reading; the more you study it, the more closely you read it, the more you will get out of it. The first reading is merely a glimpse.

Let's turn our attention to *Othello*, again Act V. Othello has made up his mind that Desdemona, his wife, whom he loves to distraction but whom he also suspects of adultery (because he has been led to this suspicion by Iago), must be killed. He enters her bedroom:

Enter Othello [with a light] and Desdemona in her bed.

Othello: It is the cause, it is the cause, my soul.
Let me not name it to you, you chaste stars.
It is the cause. Yet I'll not shed her blood,
Nor scar that whiter skin of hers than snow,
And smooth as monumental alabaster.
Yet she must die, else she'll betray more men.
Put out the light, and then put out the light.
If I quench thee, thou flaming minister,
I can again thy former light restore,
Should I repent me; but once put out thy light,
Thou cunning'st pattern of excelling nature,
I know not where is that Promethean heat
That can thy light relume. When I have plucked
the rose,
I cannot give it vital growth again;
It needs must wither. I'll smell thee on the tree.

[He kisses her]

O balmy breath, that dost almost persuade
Justice to break her sword. One more, one more!
Be thus when thou art dead, and I will kill thee,
And love thee after. One more, and that's the last!
So sweet was ne'er so fatal. I must weep,
But they are cruel tears. This sorrow's heavenly;
It strikes where it doth love. She wakes.

Again, notice the rhythm: five feet to a line, each foot *weak strong*. (We call this rhythm *iambic pentameter*.) You try to work out the rhythm of the following line:

It is the cause, it is the cause, my soul.

29

Yes, you are right:

$$\smile \diagup \smile \quad \diagup \quad \smile \diagup \smile \quad \diagup \quad \smile \diagup$$

It is the cause, it is the cause, my soul

and you are right again when you say this rhythm is iambic pentameter. Try the next five lines. Yes, you are right again. (This is easy, isn't it?) It is all iambic pentameter, but in line 5 "alabaster" breaks the rhythm and therefore alters the pace. Then the rhythm returns to iambic pentamenter. When is the rhythm broken again? Now look for the images. In *Macbeth* we found time images: what are the images here, and which words carry these images? Obviously he is carrying a candle for light: how is that candle image used, and what effect does it create?

Shakespeare also wrote many sonnets. The sonnet is a kind of framework with a fixed number of lines (fourteen, in fact) a fixed rhythm and a fixed rhyme scheme. What he wants to say has to fit into this framework. Read carefully the following sonnet, perhaps one of his most famous:

Shall I compare thee to a Summer's day?	*a*
Thou art more lovely and more temperate:	*b*
Rough winds do shake the darling buds of May,	*a*
And Summer's lease hath all too short a date:	*b*
Sometime too hot the eye of heaven shines,	*c*
And often is his god complexion dimm'd;	*d*
And every fair from fair sometime declines,	*c*
By chance or nature's changing course untrimm'd:	*d*
But thy eternal Summer shall not fade	*e*
Nor lose possession of that fair thou owest;	*f*
Nor shall Death brag thou wanderest in his shade,	*e*
When in eternal lines to time thou growest:	*f*
So long as men can breathe, or eyes can see,	*g*
So long lives this, and this gives life to thee.	*g*

There are, then, fourteen lines — 12 + 2. The rhyme scheme is *a b a b c d c d e f e f g g* : the final two are what we call a rhyming couplet. The rhythm is iambic pentameter. But the sonnet is very dense — richly packed. He takes a central image — the comparison of the person to a summer's day

30

— and exploits that image throughout the sonnet. Firstly, he explores what can be imperfect about a summer's day, then he suggests that the person's summer-like beauty cannot fade, and death cannot claim its victory. The explanation comes in the couplet: as long as human beings exist and as long as Shakespeare's poem exists, then the person's beauty must also continue to exist since his beauty is immortalised in the poetry. It's technically quite stunning; but more to the point, Shakespeare was right: four hundred years later the poem is still in existence and you, the reader, have just re-created the person's beauty since you have just read the poem.

Shakespeare lived for most of his life in the first Elizabethan age. Elizabeth I was a powerful, formidable woman, who died in 1603 having left no heir to the throne of England. Her cousin, Mary Queen of Scots, did have a claim to the throne, but Elizabeth had had her executed in 1587. Part of the problem had been that Mary was a Roman Catholic, and thus unacceptable as a monarch of England. However, Mary's son, James VI of Scotland, had been brought up a Protestant, and it was he who was sent for on the death of Elizabeth, to be James the First of the United Kingdom of England and Scotland, thus beginning the troubled reign of the House of Stuart. Shakespeare was writing at the time of the Union, and, indeed, *Macbeth* was written (most probably) for the benefit of the theatre-loving king, who was descended from the noble Banquo.

Shakespeare may have died on 23rd April, 1616, but his contribution to poetry has lived on and his influence is still felt at the end of the 20th century. He is, in a sense, inescapable, and only the uninformed or the prejudiced would attempt to deny his genius.

The poets whom we think of as following Shakespeare were, many of them, really his contemporaries. They are known to us as "Metaphysical Poets", the most famous of whom is probably John Donne. One of the most astonishing aspects of the Metaphysical Poets is that their poetry sounds very modern, almost twentieth century, though the spelling reveals their seventeenth century background. The term "metaphysical" should not unduly worry you, partly because it is too complex to explain here and partly because it is only a label and labels are often off-putting. The label was not applied to them until long after they were dead, and when it was applied it was intended as a kind of affectionate mocking. Suffice it to say, that it indicates that these poets had a fondness for indulging in philosophy in its widest sense. They had a knack for seeing the philosophical in almost any context.

We have actually already looked at a metaphysical poem, or rather a poem by a metaphysical poet, on page 9 called *To Daffodils*. It illustrates what I mean: the poet, while talking about daffodils, is also reflecting on the brevity of life. John Donne (1572 – 1631) did much to develop the technique of extended metaphor or "conceit". Let me explain what the term means. A metaphor is when you say that one thing can be thought of in terms of another: "Kevin was a lion in the fight" — in other words Kevin wasn't actually a lion but fought with lion-like qualities, such as courage, bravery, ferocity, etcetera. If you think of Kevin as "A" and the lion-like qualities as "B", then "A" is described in terms of "B" so that we know something more about "A" (i.e. his "B-like" qualities). But the metaphor tells us nothing about "B" itself: it isn't thought of as having "A-like" qualities.

Now a "conceit" does go that bit further. It describes "A" in terms of "B", but also, in the very development of the image, "B" is being explored in itself and, sometimes, in terms of "A". This is clearer when you look at one of his poems:

THE SUNNE RISING

BUSIE old foole, unruly Sunne,
　　　Why dost thou thus,
Through windowes, and through curtaines call on us?
Must to thy motions lovers seasons run?
　　　Sawey pedantique wretch, goe chide
　　　Late schoole boyes, and sowre prentices,
　　Goe tell Court-huntsmen, that the King will ride.
Call countrey ants to harvest offices;
Love, all alike, no season knowes, nor clyme,
Nor houres, dayes, moneths, which are the rags of time

　　　Thy beames, so reverend, and strong
　　　Why shouldst thou thinke?
I could eclipse and cloud them with a winke.

32

But that I would not lose her sight so long:
                If her eyes have not blinded thine,
                Looke, and to morrow late, tell mee,
        Whether both the 'India's of spice and Myne
        Be where thou leftst them, or lie here with mee.
Aske for those Kings whom thou saw'st yesterday,
And thou shalt heare, All here in one bed lay.

                She'is all States, and all Princes, I,
                Nothing else is.
Princes doe but play us; compar'd to this,
All honor's mimique; All wealth alchimie,
        Thou sunne art halfe as happy'as wee,
        In that the world's contracted thus;
        Thine age askes ease, and since thy duties bee
        To warme the world, that's done in warming us.
Shine here to us, and thou art every where;
This bed thy centre is, these walls, thy spheare.

As with Chaucer, leave the consonants, drop the final "e" and alter the vowels and, usually, you will recognise the word: thus "sowre" is "sour".

Now this is a perfect example of the conceit. The lovers are being compared to the sun. It is treated as being a pedantic intruder into their arrogant love. The lovers, being superior, do not have to fit in to the seasons of the sun. It controls time — useful to those with petty jobs — whereas theirs is a timeless existence. Verse two suggests that the lovers are more powerful than the sun:

                Thy beames, so reverend, and strong
                Why shouldst thou thinke?
        I could eclipse and cloud them with a winke,
        But that I would not lose her sight so long:
                If her eyes have not blinded thine.

It is such a clever image: for all that the sun is supposed to be strong, the poet can shut out the sunlight with a wink, except that in so doing he would lose sight of his lover for that second. In any case, the brightness of her eyes blinds the sunlight. You can see how the metaphor is continually developed with such words as "eclipse" and "cloud" — all words we associate with the sun. The arrogance in the next few lines is built up: he tells the sun (by implication) to go off round the world and, in twenty-four hours, "tomorrow late", tell him if "both the'India's" be where "thou leftst them" or, indeed, if they be here with him. In other words, all the riches associated with "the'India's" are here beside him in bed.

He goes on:

> Aske for those kings whom thou saw'st yesterday,
> And thou shalt heare, All here in one bed lay.

If she is all the riches in the world, he is all the power. Of all the kings the sun sees in the world, he is the most powerful. The idea is continued into the next verse. In comparison to them all honour is mimicry, all wealth alchemy (in the seventeenth century scientists devoted much energy in trying to make gold out of lead, a process never successful, but referred to as "alchemy"). He, flippantly, patronises the sun by saying that since it is old, all it has to do is warm their bed and not the whole world. In warming them, it is in effect warming the whole world because "This bed thy centre is".

Do you get the idea of the conceit? In comparing their love to the sun, the poet is also exploring ideas about the sun itself. The lovers are not just self-centred, they are sun-centred.

The rhyme scheme — *a b b a c d c d e e* — is complex and tight, and the rhythm is complex but regular, all of which, combined with the sharpness of the ideas, makes for a very clever poem, intellectually bright, yet witty. That cleverness is further illustrated in *The Anniversarie*, another love poem:

THE ANNIVERSARIE

> ALL Kings, and all their favourites,
> All glory of honors, beauties, wits,
> The Sun it selfe, which makes times, as they passe,

Is elder by a yeare, now, than it was
When thou and I first one another saw:
All other things, to their destruction draw,
   Only our love hath no decay;
This, no to morrow hath, nor yesterday,
Running it never runs from us away,
But truly keepes, his first, last, everlasting day.

   Two graves must hide thine and my coarse
   If one might, death were no divorce.
Alas, as well as other Princes, wee,
(Who Prince enough in one another bee,)
Must leave at last in death, these eyes, and eares,
Oft fed with true oathes, and with sweet salt teares;
   But soules where nothing dwells but love
(All other thoughts being inmates) then shall prove
This, or a love increased there above,
When bodies to their graves, soules from their
   graves remove.

   And then wee shall be throughly blest,
   But wee no more, than all the rest;
Here upon earth, we'are Kings, and none but wee
Can be such Kings, nor of such subjects bee.
Who is so safe as wee? where none can doe
Treason to us, except one of us two.
   True and false feares let us refrain,
Let us love nobly, and live, and adde againe
Yeares and yeares unto yeares, till we attaine
To write threescore: this is the second of our raigne.

JOHN DONNE

This poem, though less amusing than *The Sunne Rising*, is still very appealing intellectually because of the cleverness of the ideas and of the techniques that Donne uses. His concern is the concept of time: all things, kings, honour, beauty, wit, even the sun, are subject to time and therefore to decay; all things, that is, except for their love. It is one year since the lovers met and everything has grown one year more in decay but not their love. It is not subject to time. But look how Donne uses rhythm to express the idea: compare the rhythm of the second line, "All glory of honors, beauties, wits", with the seventh line, "Only our love hath no decay", and you will see what I mean. The second line has a staccato, quick, jerky rhythm whereas the seventh line has a slow, almost melifluous, flow to it. The former is achieved by the hard sounds — "g", "b", "t" — and short vowels, whereas the latter has long vowel sounds and no hard consonants. Note also his use of repetition in the next three lines: "Running it never runs", "his first, last, everlasting day", as well as the juxtaposition (placing side by side) of "first" and "last". Their bodies, as with all things earthy, must decay and die, but that death releases their souls, and these are where their love lives. Then they shall be blest. But, he says in verse three, it is here on earth they achieve true greatness:

> "Here upon earth, we'are Kings, and none but wee
> Can be such Kings . . ."

No other king can have such subjects; nor can they suffer treason — except at the hands of each other. They will live a long time:

> ". . . and adde againe
> Yeares and yeares unto yeares, till we attaine
> To write threescore: . . ."

The bit after the colon is what brings the entire poem suddenly and startingly to a sharp climax:

> ". . . this is the second of our raigne."

a reminder not only of the title and the beginning of the poem, but a celebration of the fact that, for them, it's only just beginning. Again there is this marvellous build up of years and years to the total of 60 years, then the sudden juxtaposition of this being only the second year. "Raigne" or "reign" seems particularly apposite.

– VI –

SEVENTEENTH AND EIGHTEENTH CENTURIES

The Jacobean Period (1603 – 1625) ("Jacobean" is used to describe the period of James's reign, as "Elizabethan" is used to describe the reign of Elizabeth) was a highly prolific period in terms of literature: Jacobean drama, and its obsession with sex, intrigue and violence, was popular and of quality — many of the plays are still performed today. The amount of poetry being produced at this time was vast, and poems were being written by dramatists as well as poets. If the Elizabethan era had been the time of Renaissance man, with his interest in art, literature, scholarship, science, geography, soldiership, fitness, then this was the time of literary man, with his fascination for writing about these things. Donne's poetry, as with the poetry of other writers of the period, reflects the discoveries of the time, especially of the New World, and reflects also the continuing obsession with kingship. The interest in the King must not be confused with the gossipy noseyness of today's tabloid press about The Royals; it was an interest in power, the source of power and in government, since James, by God's annointment, was the source of these things. His power was almost absolute, unlike the Queen today whose power is, to all intents and purposes, minimal.

Let's put it this way: the seventeenth century, after the death of James I, saw the beheading of Charles I, the establishment of the Commonwealth which, between 1649 and 1660, replaced the Monarchy, the Restoration of the Stuarts, the deposing of James II and much intrigue and civil war to boot. They were heady political times. But the seventeenth century saw the emergence of the House of Commons as the seat of power. By the time the monarchy was restored, it had undergone fundamental modification, though it appeared unchanged.

The towering figure in English literature throughout this period of turmoil (and after) was John Milton (1608 – 1674). He really was highly political and a supporter of Cromwell and the Commonwealth. Even after the Restoration of Charles II in 1660, Milton's political views strengthened his reputation among young writers and intellectuals. But what established Milton's

37

reputation among the wits and scholars of the Court was his epic poem *Paradise Lost*. And that was partly because Milton made real the dream that poets had had for centuries — the dream for a truly "Christian epic".

The story of *Paradise Lost* is really the story of Adam and Eve and their expulsion from Paradise. You are unlikely ever to read all of *Paradise Lost* unless you study English Literature at university, but it is worth looking at the end of what is a very long poem. It is the point at which Adam and Eve have to leave Paradise to find their place in the world.

PARADISE LOST
Book X11 lines 625 – end.

    So spake our mother Eve; and Adam heard
Well pleased, but answered not; for now too nigh
Th' Archangel stood, and from the other hill
To their fixed station, all in bright array
The Cherubim descended, on the ground
Gliding meteorous, as evening mist,
Risen from a river, o'er the marish glides,   630
And gathers ground fast at the labourer's heel
Homeward returning. High in front advanced,
The brandished sword of God before them blazed,
Fierce as a comet, which with torrid heat,
And vapour as the Libyan air adust,
Began to parch that temperate clime; whereat
In either hand the hast'ning Angel caught
Our lingering parents, and to th' eastern gate
Led them direct, and down the cliff as fast
To the subjected plain; then disappeared.   640
They, looking back, all the eastern side beheld
Of Paradise, so late their happy seat,
Waved over by that flaming brand, the gate
With dreadful faces thronged and fiery arms:
Some natural tears they dropped, but wiped them soon;
The world was all before them, where to choose
Their place of rest, and Providence their guide:
They, hand in hand, with wandering steps and slow,
Through Eden took their solitary way.

Note the rhythm —

$$\smile \diagup \; \smile \diagup \diagup \; \smile \diagup \; \smile \; \diagup \smile \diagup$$
So spake our mother Eve; and Adam heard

— five feet in the line and each foot *weak strong*. Remember Shakespeare? And iambic pentameter? The rhythm closest to everyday speech? You remember, too, what we said about blank verse — verse which has no rhyme?

What is also interesting is the imagery Milton uses — imagery highly appropriate to the subject he is dealing with: the cataclysmic expulsion of Adam and Eve from Paradise. He captures the idea of the edge of Paradise:

> . . . in bright array
> The Cherubim descended, on the ground
> Gliding meteorous . . .

and

> . . . High in front advanced,
> The brandished sword of God before them blazed,
> Fierce as a comet . . .

Adam and Eve, on the other hand, are described as "Our lingering parents". They descend the cliff "To the subjected plain". They cry, a measure of their new-found human-ness, but they wipe the tears away, suggesting the human qualities of forbearance, and determination.

> The world was all before them, where to choose
> Their place of rest, and Providence their guide:
> They, hand in hand, with wandering steps and slow,
> Through Eden took their solitary way.

Their need to comfort each other, their uncertain direction and slow progress, their hesitancy and loneliness make them recognisably human and therefore worthy of our sympathy.

I mention all this not because you need to know about *Paradise Lost* or,

39

indeed, anything about John Milton, except that he is a major figure in English Literature and he does have his very influential place in the development of poetry.

At this time, the ballads, which we look at in Chapter IV, were being recorded in print, though of course their narratives go back much further in time. In a sense, as you can now see for yourselves, they belong in form and subject matter to a much earlier period.

The seventeenth century ends with the death of another major poet, John Dryden, whose main contribution to poetry is his biting political satire, the influence, though not the imitation, of which continues into the twentieth century. If Milton's poetry is essentially private poetry, Dryden's is written with a much wider audience in mind. This is the period we call the Augustan Age. It was a prolific period not only in terms of its poetry, but also in terms of the novel and the essay. The age was obsessed with itself, its society and its social forms. It was socially conscious. It produced Dryden, Pope, Addison, Defoe and Swift. Although you might not have heard of the authors, I'm sure you have heard of *Robinson Crusoe* and *Gulliver's Travels*.

It was an age of trade and industry, the inception perhaps of the enterprise culture which is once again so much with us. It saw the setting up of the Bank of England; insurance and trading companies such as Lloyds; the appearance of encyclopedias, and periodicals such as *The Spectator*. It was the age of the man of business who was much satirised in Defoe's writing.

The seventeenth into the eighteenth century saw the transformation of London to the modern city, the economic and cultural centre of Britain. By the end of the eighteenth century Adam Smith's *Wealth of Nations* had been published and widely read, a treatise not only influential then but which has so much helped to shape the thinking and attitudes of the late twentieth century. If nothing else, the study of books teaches us that little changes.

One of the writers of this period, whom I much enjoy reading, is Alexander Pope (1688 – 1744). His poetry is much concerned with society and social behaviour, but it's really his style I like. He is bitingly satirical and, at times, downright funny. But, you comment, there are those words again: "Satire", "satirical". What do they mean? A good question and one which is difficult to answer. "Satire" is a word really in the same class as "metaphor" and "irony" — we kind of know how to use these words but find it difficult to say what they mean. Let's leave "metaphor" aside for a moment and come back to it later — "put it on the back burner", to use one of the most tired-out, clichéd metaphors that are around these days.

"Irony" and "Satire" are linked. Irony is when two (or more) situations, events, occurrences, words, ideas are brought together in such a way that one implies a comment on the other. Someone present, but not everybody, is sufficiently intelligent and sensitive to be aware of the comment, and to realise that the comment involves something contradictory that is sometimes amusing and always significant. For example, I can remember one day in Primary 7 when we had what was called Religious Education. That usually involved the teacher, a small, fierce, humourless woman, setting us bits of the bible to learn by heart (as homework) to be tested the following day. The test comprised of her pointing at some poor soul, who had to stand up and recite the said piece faultlessly and unhesitatingly. One day she told us to learn Corinthians XIII: "Though I speak with the tongues of men and of angels and have not charity . . . and now abideth faith, hope, charity, these three, but the greatest of these is charity." None of us had a clue what the piece meant, but that bothered the teacher not a bit — though it did make learning by heart all the more difficult. Part of the exercise, no doubt. I discovered that night, however, that "charity" in 1611 (when the bible was translated at James I's behest) meant love; so the piece was all about the power of love, which can move mountains and bring about forgiveness. In class the next day, one boy was pointed at; he got up, and he stammered and stumbled through the first few lines until charity died on his lips. He was taken out and soundly thrashed for his stupidity and idleness. But the point wasn't lost on me: in my eleven year-old way it struck me as more than odd that this child was being soundly beaten for not having been able to recite something about love. It was more than odd — it was ironic. Here were the two events — the inability to quote from the bible about the nature of love and the beating by the teacher — and the one event commented on the other because of the contradiction; it was both amusing to us and significant to him. Of one thing I am certain: the irony was totally lost on the teacher.

Irony, at a simpler level, can be the device of saying one thing while

41

meaning the opposite, though that is closer to sarcasm especially if ridicule is intended. Satire is like that: it is where stupidity or pomposity or arrogance or self-importance is being challenged by being held up to ridicule. And the Augustan writers were superb at satire. You should try reading *Gulliver's Travels*, which is not a book for children, but is really a very clever and funny ridicule of the prevailing economic climate of the time.

But to return to Pope, who was a satirist, particularly incisive in his ridicule of the social manners of the early eighteenth century. One thing you have to know though: like Milton, but unlike Shakespeare, Pope was writing for a highly-educated, highly-sophisticated, cultivated audience, and therefore much of what he wrote has less of an appeal today than, say, the plays of Shakespeare. To appreciate Pope you have to know something of the age in which and for which he was writing, thus his writing can have a 'dated' feel. That his poetry is still read, however, is a tribute to the man's genius and to the fact that his work, however topical, nevertheless has universal appeal.

His most famous poem, perhaps, is *The Rape of the Lock*, which ridicules the fashionable and socially-conscious world in which Pope lived. If *Paradise Lost* is a truly epic poem dealing with massively universal and significant themes, then *The Rape of the Lock* is a mock-heroic poem which outwardly appears to be dealing with themes of epic proportions but actually deals with the trivial and the mundane. He achieves this by writing about the frivolous in the epic style, and the result is both amusing and bitingly critical. One of the best known excerpts from the poem is the beginning of Canto III:

THE RAPE OF THE LOCK

CANTO III

Close by those Meads for ever crown'd with Flow'rs,
Where *Thames* with Pride surveys his rising Tow'rs,
There stands a Structure of Majestick Frame,
Which from the neighb'ring *Hampton* takes its Name.
Here *Britain's* Statesmen oft the fall foredoom   5
Of Foreign Tyrants, and of Nymphs at home;
Here Thou, Great *Anna*! whom three Realms obey,
Dost sometimes Counsel take — and sometimes *Tea*.
    Hither the Heroes and the Nymphs resort,

To taste awhile the Pleasures of a Court;   10
In various Talk th' instructive hours they past,
Who gave the *Ball*, or paid the *Visit* last:
One speaks the Glory of the *British Queen*,
And one describes a charming *Indian Screen*;
A third interprets Motions, Looks, and Eyes;   15
At ev'ry Word a reputation dies.
Snuff, or the *Fan*, supply each Pause of Chat,
With singing, laughing, ogling, and all that.

We have talked about iambic pentameter — note that once again it is present — and we have talked about the rhyming couplet — *a a b b c c* — and here the combination of the rhythm and rhyme creates a humorous effect. But Pope achieves his mocking tone by using anti-climax. Climax is a device used in poetry and drama whereby the writer builds up tension almost to breaking point. A perfect example is the build-up to the climax of the murder of Duncan in *Macbeth* right to the point where Macbeth exclaims:

Wake Duncan with thy knocking! I would thou couldst!

by which point the audience (and Macbeth) can take no more. Anti-climax is the opposite effect: there is still the build-up to a point, and then the writer craftily and often wittily lets you down by puncturing the tension.

Close by those Meads for ever crown'd with Flow'rs,
Where *Thames* with Pride surveys his rising Tow'rs,
There stands a Structure of Majestick Frame,
Which from the neighb'ring *Hampton* takes its Name.
Here *Britain's* Statesmen oft the fall foredoom
Of Foreign Tyrants, and of Nymphs at home;
Here Thou, Great *Anna*! whom three Realms obey,
Dost sometimes Counsel take — and sometimes *Tea*.

There is the build-up to "great *Anna*", and note the contribution of the use of italic letters to that build-up, the continuation of the climax by the statements that three realms obey her and that she sometimes seeks advice. Then the let down: as well as taking counsel to help her in her imperious position she also takes tea. Even the use of para-rhyme or near rhyme ("obey" and "tea") adds to the humour.

It is the humour which perhaps we most appreciate when we read *The Rape of the Lock* today — a humour which, in its witty, clever, articulate and biting way, is very much in keeping with our age. You are unlikely to read the whole poem, but do try to read bits of it. As an educated reader yourself, you ought to know something about Alexander Pope, something of the Augustans, and something of the Eighteenth Century. This chapter has tried to set you on your way.

– VII –

NINETEENTH CENTURY

The division of the millenium into centuries is obviously useful for all kinds of reasons, but the development of poetry doesn't really lend itself to the precision of chronometry. Yet we are so conditioned to think in centuries that we lump the Augustans into the eighteenth century and the Romantics into the nineteenth. That the Augustan period probably ended before the eighteenth century was fifty years old, and that Wordsworth, the first of the first generation of Romantic poets, was born in 1770, are awkward little facts that render the century boundary almost meaningless.

Nevertheless, the characteristics of Augustan poetry, intellect, wit, social commentary continued on to the end of the century in a more arid and esoteric form. The language of the late eighteenth century poets became obscure, convoluted, obtuse. Cleverness was all-important. Their interests were rational: that is, the mind, science and politics were their subject matters. The world of emotion, of feelings, of everyday occurrences were of no consequence. They certainly had little interest in the inward world of the poet and none in landscape.

To those attitudes came a reaction, and three poets in particular — Blake, Wordsworth and Coleridge — began to anticipate the trend to come. Their concerns were the insights of childhood, the world of inner self, mystery and fantasy, and, of course, the world of nature. The emphasis shifted from the classical and critical to the passionate and creative.

Of the three first generation Romantic poets, you are probably most aware of Wordsworth. If I tell you William Blake wrote *The Tyger* —

> Tyger! Tyger! burning bright
> In the forests of the night

— then there might be a flash of recognition. Coleridge you might have

45

heard of for his *Kubla Khan* or his *Rime of the Ancient Mariner*. But most people do know the name William Wordsworth. He wrote many, many poems, but I want to mention only one, and even then I am going to quote only the beginning and the end of it. I choose it for you because for me it captures the spirit of the thinking at the time. It is called:

ODE

INTIMATIONS OF IMMORTALITY FROM
RECOLLECTIONS OF EARLY CHILDHOOD

It indicates the shift from the arid intellectual wit of the middle 18th Century to the recognition of the importance of feeling and of the concerns of childhood. Here you get the child's sense of wonder and awe which a few decades on the planet tends to erode and diminish!

ODE

INTIMATIONS OF IMMORTALITY FROM
RECOLLECTIONS OF EARLY CHILDHOOD

> The Child is father of the Man;
> And I could wish my days to be
> Bound each to each by natural piety.

I

THERE was a time when meadow, grove, and stream
The earth, and every common sight,
      To me did seem
    Apparelled in celestial light,
The glory and the freshness of a dream.
It is not now as it hath been of yore; —
      Turn wheresoe'er I may
      By night or day,
The things which I have seen I now can see no more.

II

10

The Rainbow comes and goes,
And lovely is the Rose,
The moon doth with delight
Look round her when the heavens are bare,
Waters on a starry night
Are beautiful and fair;
The sunshine is a glorious birth;
But yet I know, where'er I go,
That there hath past away a glory from the earth.

XI

And O, ye Fountains, Meadows, Hills, and Groves,
Forebode not any severing of our loves!
Yet in my heart of hearts I feel your might;
I only have relinquished one delight   190
To live beneath your more habitual sway.
I love the Brooks which down their channels fret,
Even more than when I tripped lightly as they;
The innocent brightness of a new-born Day
                    Is lovely yet;
The Clouds that gather round the setting sun
Do take a sober colouring from an eye
That hath kept watch o'er man's mortality;
Another race hath been, and other palms are won.
Thanks to the human heart by which we live,   200
Thanks to its tenderness, its joys, and fears,
To me the meanest flower that blows can give
Thoughts that do often lie too deep for tears.

WILLIAM WORDSWORTH

You can detect right away the difference in subject matter and in language. This poem is easier to follow than Pope's *Rape of the Lock*. The whole poem is quite long — some 200 lines — but what it says is straightforward enough: childhood gives us glimpses of eternal truths, whereas adulthood ("down to palsied Age") makes us jaded and less perceptive. By recollecting childhood, the poet can get back to the real, true perceptions of things to such an extent that the meanest flower can give him thoughts that lie too deep for tears.

The second generation of Romantic poets are Shelly, Byron, Keats and Tennyson. Of these poets, Keats features in the new Revised Higher since certain of his poems — *The Eve of St. Agnes*, *Ode to a Nightingale*, *Ode to Autumn*, *Bright Star!*, *When I have Fears* . . . and *La Belle Dame sans Merci* — are Set Texts. Keats was born at the very end of the eighteenth century (1795) and died a very young man in 1821. Keats wrote his odes in 1819 by which time he had become a very able and mature poet. By this point, and in *Ode to Autumn* in particular, he exemplifies all that is best in Romantic poetry — entirely original responses to first-hand experiences. When you are reading Keats it is vital to keep in mind the idea of "original responses" or, at least, "genuine" responses. It is all too easy to slip into the habit of reading English literature notes, thereby forming not your own reaction to the poem but an amalgam of other critics' reactions.

ODE TO A NIGHTINGALE

I

My heart aches, and a drowsy numbness pains
    My sense, as though of hemlock I had drunk,
Or emptied some dull opiate to the drains
    One minute past, and Lethe-wards had sunk:
'Tis not through envy of thy happy lot,
    But being too happy in thine happiness, —
        That thou, light-winged Dryad of the trees,
        In some melodious plot
Of beechen green, and shadows numberless,
    Singest of summer in full-throated ease.

II

O, for a draught of vintage! that hath been
    Cool'd a long age in the deep-delved earth,
Tasting of Flora and the country green,
    Dance, and Provençal song, and sunburnt mirth!

O for a beaker full of the warm South,
    Full of the true, the blushful Hippocrene,
        With beaded bubbles winking at the brim,
           And purple-stained mouth;
That I might drink, and leave the world unseen,
        And with thee fade away into the forest dim:

III

Fade far away, dissolve, and quite forget
    What thou among the leaves hast never known,
The weariness, the fever, and the fret
    Here, where men sit and hear each other groan;
Where palsy shakes a few, sad, last gray hairs,
        Where youth grows pale, and spectre-thin, and dies;
           Where but to think is to be full of sorrow
              And leaden-eyed despairs,
Where Beauty cannot keep her lustrous eyes,
    Or new Love pine at them beyond to-morrow.

IV

Away! away! for I will fly to thee,
    Not charioted by Bacchus and his pards,
But on the viewless wings of Poesy,
    Though the dull brain perplexes and retards:
Already with thee! tender is the night,
      And haply the Queen-Moon is on her throne,
        Cluster'd around by all her starry Fays;
          But here there is no light,
Save what from heaven is with the breezes blown
      Through verdurous glooms and winding mossy
        ways.

V

I cannot see what flowers are at my feet,
    Nor what soft incense hangs upon the boughs,
But, in embalmed darkness, guess each sweet
    Wherewith the seasonable month endows
The grass, the thicket, and the fruit-tree wild;

White hawthorn, and the pastoral eglantine;
　　Fast fading violets cover'd up in leaves;
　　　　And mid-May's eldest child,
The coming musk-rose, full of dewy wine,
　　The murmurous haunt of flies on summer eves.

VI

Darkling I listen; and, for many a time
　　I have been half in love with easeful Death,
Call'd him soft names in many a mused rhyme,
　　To take into the air my quiet breath;
Now more than ever seems it rich to die,
　　To cease upon the midnight with no pain,
　　　　While thou art pouring forth thy soul abroad
　　　　　　In such an ecstasy!
Still wouldst thou sing, and I have ears in vain —
　　To thy high requiem become a sod.

VII

Thou wast not born for death, immortal Bird!
　　No hungry generations tread thee down;
The voice I hear this passing night was heard
　　In ancient days by emperor and clown:
Perhaps the self-same song that found a path
　　Through the sad heart of Ruth, when, sick for home,
　　　　She stood in tears amid the alien corn;
　　　　　　The same that oft-times hath
Charm'd magic casements, opening on the foam
　　Of perilous seas, in faery lands forlorn

VIII

Forlorn! the very word is like a bell
　　To toll me back from thee to my sole self!
Adieu! the fancy cannot cheat so well
　　As she is fam'd to do, deceiving elf.
Adieu! adieu! thy plaintive anthem fades
　　Past the near meadows, over the still stream,
　　　　Up the hill-side; and now 'tis buried deep
　　　　　　In the next valley-glades:
Was it a vision, or a waking dream?
　　Fled is that music: — Do I wake or sleep?

Remember from your reading of *The Practical Guide to Literature* the three questions to ask yourself about any work of art:

(a) What is the poem about?

(b) What effects does it have on me?

(c) How have these effects been achieved?

This technique applies as much to the poetry of the pre-twentieth century as it does to the kind of poetry you are perhaps more in the habit of studying. What is *Ode to a Nightingale* about? Perhaps you need to know that Keats wrote this poem after the death of his younger brother. It is obviously about the poet's feelings and about what the nightingale represents for him and to him. How do you feel when you read it? Sad, thoughtful, sympathetic? How has the poet made you feel that way? What techniques has he used? Look carefully at the first verse:

> My heart aches, and a drowsy numbness pains
>> My sense, as though of hemlock I had drunk,
> Or emptied some dull opiate to the drains
>> One minute past, and Lethe-wards had sunk:
> 'Tis not through envy of thy happy lot,
>> But being too happy in thine happiness, —
>>> That thou, light-winged Dryad of the trees,
>>> In some melodious plot
> Of beechen green, and shadows numberless,
>>> Singest of summer in full-throated ease.

First of all, examine the rhyme-scheme — what do you notice? *a b a b c d e c d e* : what effect does such a rhyme-scheme have? Look at the rhymes themselves, especially "happiness" with "numberless". Almost you don't notice the rhyme until you look for it. Notice the number of long vowel sounds: what effect do they have? (See *Practical Guide to Literature* by David Cockburn, published by Robert Gibson & Sons, page 23.) Some words you may be uncertain of: "hemlock", "Lethe", "Dryad" — look them up in a dictionary. To save you too much hunting a dryad was, according to the ancient Greeks, a nymph of the trees who, it was thought, died in the trees. Listen to the alliteration of the "s" sound in the last four verses — again what is the effect and in what way is the sound appropriate?

You can go through the whole poem asking yourself these questions. You will begin to appreciate how technically excellent this poem is. It explores feelings but not in any indulgent, conceited, self-satisfied way.

Keats died, aged 26, of tuberculosis: a very common cause of death in the 19th and early 20th centuries. Many people died young — medicine was at an embryonic stage and antibiotics didn't exist at all. Look at verse three of *Ode to a Nightingale*:

> Where palsy shakes a few, sad, last grey hairs,
>> Where youth grows pale, and spectre-thin, and dies;

"Spectre-thin" refers to one of the symptoms of tuberculosis — but why does he choose to say "spectre-thin" rather than, say, "very thin"? What does the word "spectre" add? Keats is a very typical romantic poet; not only do his poems have all the characteristics of romantic poetry, but, like Byron, his very life-story was romantic as was his death in Rome in November 1821.

Lord Tennyson (1809 – 1892) experienced most of the 19th century, and is, perhaps, a poet a little too under-rated today. He wrote some magnificent poems and so doing breathed life into some ancient legends, giving them a relevance and an excitement not only for the Victorian era, but for ourselves poised as we are on the verge of a new millenium.

Morte d'Arthur you may not have read, but you will have heard of King Arthur, the Round Table, and sword Excalibur. In this poem, Tennyson describes the death of Arthur, the return of his sword to the lake from whence it came, and the end of an era.

Here are two extracts from the poem. The first extract portrays the dying Arthur who has charged his knight, Sir Bedivere, with the duty of throwing Excalibur, his sword, back into the lake from which, one summer noon, he had taken it. It had been offered him by an arm, clothed in white samite, risen up from the middle of the lake. Now he wanted Sir Bedivere to return the sword to the lake. Twice Sir Bedivere pretended to have returned the sword, but each time Arthur knew that the knight had lied. At the third attempt Sir Bedivere threw the sword, which:

> Made lightnings in the splendour of the moon,
> And flashing round and round, and whirl'd in an arch,
> Shot like a streamer of the northern morn,
> Seen where the moving isles of winter shock   140
> By night, with noises of the northern sea.
> So flash'd and fell the brand Excalibur:
> But ere he dipt the surface, rose an arm
> Clothed in white samite, mystic, wonderful,
> And caught him by the hilt, and brandish'd him
> Three times, and drew him under in the mere.
> And lightly went the other to the King.
>   Then spoke King Arthur, drawing thicker breath:
> 'Now see I by thine eyes that this is done.
> Speak out: what is it thou hast heard or seen?'   150
>   And answer made the bold Sir Bedivere:
> 'Sir King, I closed mine eyelids, lest the gems
> Should blind my purpose, for I never saw,
> Nor shall see, here or elsewhere, till I die,
> Not tho' I live three lives of mortal men,
> So great a miracle as yonder hilt.

After that, a barge came to take Arthur away, leaving Bedivere behind.

> Then loudly cried the bold Sir Bedivere,
> 'Ah! my Lord Arthur, whither shall I go?
> Where shall I hide my forehead and my eyes?
> For now I see the true old times are dead,
> When every morning brought a noble chance,   230
> And every chance brought out a noble knight.
> Such times have been not since the light that led
> The holy Elders with the gift of myrrh.
> But now the whole ROUND TABLE is dissolved
> Which was an image of the mighty world;

53

And I, the last, go forth companionless
And the days darken round me, and the years,
Among new men, strange faces, other minds.'
        And slowly answer'd Arthur from the barge:
'The old order changeth, yielding place to new,   240
And God fulfils Himself in many ways,
Lest one good custom should corrupt the world.
Comfort thyself: what comfort is in me?
I have lived my life, and that which I have done
May He within Himself make pure! but thou,
If thou shouldst never see my face again,
Pray for my soul. More things are wrought by prayer
Than this world dreams of. Wherefore, let they voice
Rise like a fountain for me night and day.
For what are men better than sheep or goats   250
That nourish a blind life within the brain,
If, knowing God, they lift not hands of prayer
Both for themselves and those who call them friend?
For so the whole round earth is every way
Bound by gold chains about the feet of God.
But now farewell. I am going a long way
With these thou seëst — if indeed I go —
(For all my mind is clouded with a doubt)
To the island-valley of Avilion;
Where falls not hail, or rain, or any snow,   260
Nor ever wind blows loudly; but it lies
Deep-meadow'd, happy, fair with orchard-lawns
And bowery hollows crown'd with summer sea,
Where I will heal me of my grievous wound.'
        So said he, and the barge with oar and sail
Moved from the brink, like some full-breasted swan
That, fluting a wild carol ere her death,
Ruffles her pure cold plume, and takes the flood
With swarthy webs. Long stood Sir Bedivere
Revolving many memories, till the hull   270
Look'd one black dot against the verge of dawn,
And on the mere the wailing died away.

LORD TENNYSON

I think you will agree even from this small fragment that this is a very easy
poem to read. There are none of the obscurities so characteristic of much

modern poetry, none of the difficulties of language, none of the opacities of meaning. It is a straightforward, narrative poem which excels in its clarity of meaning and lucidity of language. No need to spend long on the question "What is the poem about?"; not really any need to spend any longer on the question "What effects does it have on me?"; but we can spend many hours examining just how these effects have been achieved. It is a technical masterpiece: Tennyson exploits all kinds of devices of structure, rhythm and sound, imagery, connotation. It is a very rich poem, powerfully written, and very appealing to our imaginations. Anyone who reads it sensitively and appreciatively cannot but be struck by his use of onomatopoeia — the device whereby an author uses a word or words associated with the sound being described: e.g. "bang". Look at the following lines:

> He heard the deep behind him, and a cry
> Before. His own thought drove him like a goad.
> Dry clash'd his harness in the icy caves
> And barren chasms, and all to left and right
> The bare black cliff clang'd round him, as he based
> His feet on juts of slippery crag that rang
> Sharp-smitten with the dint of armed heels —

You can see — hear — what I mean: words such as "cry", "clash'd", "chasms", "clang'd", "crag", "rang", "sharp-smitten", "dint". But there are all kinds of examples of such onomatopoeic words throughout the poem. Alliteration, very much related to onomatopoeia, is also much in evidence: "bare black", "sharp-smitten", "cliff-clanged".

There is a highly dramatic, ringing quality to this poem. The language is very grand, without being overblown or over the top. Look at lines 240 – 242:

> 'The old order changeth, yielding place to new,
> And God fulfils Himself in many ways,
> Lest one good custom should corrupt the world'.

— a theme which, in a sense, is picked up in *Ulysses*.

ULYSSES

It little profits that an idle king,
By this still hearth, among these barren crags,
Match'd with an aged wife, I mete and dole
Unequal laws unto a savage race,
That hoard, and sleep, and feed, and know not me.
I cannot rest from travel: I will drink
Life to the lees: all times I have enjoy'd
Greatly, have suffer'd greatly, both with those
That loved me, and alone; on shore, and when
Thro' scudding drifts the rainy Hyades   10
Vext the dim sea: I am become a name;
For always roaming with a hungry heart
Much have I seen and known; cities of men
And manners, climates, councils, governments,
Myself not least, but honour'd of them all;
And drunk delight of battle with my peers,
Far on the ringing plains of windy Troy.
I am a part of all that I have met;
Yet all experience is an arch wherethro'
Gleams that untravell'd world, whose margin fades   20
For ever and for ever when I move.
How dull it is to pause, to make an end,
To rust unburnish'd, not to shine in use!
As tho' to breathe were life. Life piled on life
Were all too little, and of one to me
Little remains: but every hour is saved
From that eternal silence, something more,
A bringer of new things; and vile it were
For some three suns to store and hoard myself,
And this grey spirit yearning in desire   30
To follow knowledge, like a sinking star,
Beyone the utmost bound of human thought.
            This is my son, mine own Telemachus,
To whom I leave the sceptre and the isle —
Well-loved of me, discerning to fulfil
This labour, by slow prudence to make mild
A rugged people, and thro' soft degrees
Subdue them to the useful and the good.
Most blameless is he, centred in the sphere

Of common duties, decent not to fail   40
In offices of tenderness, and pay
Meet adoration to my household gods,
When I am gone. He works his work, I mine.
                    There lies the port: the vessel puffs her sail:
There gloom the dark broad seas. My mariners,
Souls that have toil'd, and wrought, and thought with me —
That ever with a frolic welcome took
The thunder and the sunshine, and opposed
Free hearts, free foreheads — you and I are old;
Old age hath yet his honour and his toil;   50
Death closes all: but something ere the end,
Some work of noble note, may yet be done,
Not unbecoming men that strove with Gods.
The lights begin to twinkle from the rocks:
The long day wanes: the slow moon climbs: the deep
Moans round with many voices. Come, my friends,
'Tis not too late to seek a newer world.
Push off, and sitting well in order smite
The sounding furrows; for my purpose holds
To sail beyond the sunset, and the baths   60
Of all the western stars, until I die.
It may be that the gulfs will wash us down:
It may be we shall touch the Happy Isles,
And see the great Achilles, whom we knew.
Tho' much is taken, much abides; and tho'
We are not now that strength which in old days
Moved earth and heaven; that which we are, we are;
One equal temper of heroic hearts,
Made weak by time and fate, but strong in will
To strive, to seek, to find, and not to yield.   70

The ending of this poem, like the ending of *Morte D'Arthur*, explores the notion of the old order giving way to the new. Read again lines 56 – 70 and you will see what I mean — although here the idea is expressed in terms of the exploration of the new. We talked about anti-climax when we examined Pope's *Rape of the Lock*; here we have the perfect example of climax —

                              . . . but strong in will
          To strive, to seek, to find, and not to yield.

Inspiring thoughts!

Ulysses, or to give him his Greek name, Odysseus, was one of the many suitors to Helen of Troy and, as such, played a major and valiant part in the Trojan war. On his way back from Troy, he underwent many adventures, recounted in Homer's *Odyssey*. He had been unsuccessful in marrying Helen, and instead married Penelope, who had waited for him during the twenty years it had taken him to return home to her in Ithaca from Troy. He lived for sixteen years in Ithaca, eventually being killed unwittingly by his son, Telegonus. Tennyson's monologue, not part of Homer's story, is set in Ulysses' last years.

One of the points I'd want to make about this poem is that it is a monologue. Ulysses, himself, is speaking throughout the poem; and a poem in which the poet assumes the character of someone else, and writes it in such a way that the reader thinks that the character is speaking, we call a "monologue", sometimes a "dramatic monologue". We will look at another dramatic monologue in the next chapter. In the meantime, ask yourself what Tennyson reveals about Ulysses. What does the poet gain by choosing to write the poem in this way?

Remember that the way in to any poem (or play, or novel, or television drama, or film) is to ask 'What is it about?' The answer to that question will give you the theme or themes of the work you are studying. Well, what is this poem about? Read it over again, and I think you will be amazed at the number of answers to the question you can supply. It is spoken by an old man who had been very active, adventurous and successful. You need to imagine what that must be like: to be a hero without, any longer, the ability to be heroic. To be, in a sense, retired. After you've sorted out all themes, you then need to think about the *effect* the poem had on you. This poem can make you feel thrilled, noble, almost zealous. How does Tennyson create that feeling. Look carefully at the language — has it any heroic qualities? Look at the images and ask yourself if they are appropriate. "I will drink/Life to the lees": if I tell you that the "lees" are the gritty bits left at the bottom of a bottle of good wine, can you then comment on whether it is an appropriate image? Think, also, of where the poem is set. Are there other images you can comment on? Other language features? You are beginning to get the hang of it.

– VIII –

ROBERT BURNS

I can't really write a book which deals, however briefly, with the history of English poetry without mentioning something about Robert Burns. Scottish poetry, in a sense, is not part of the mainstream of English poetry. The Scots have always had a problem forced upon them partly by the Union of the Crowns in 1603 and partly by the Union of Parliaments in 1707: language. The Scots somehow lost confidence in themselves by the devolvement of power, both political and intellectual, to London. That loss of confidence was, and probably still is, most noticeable in our attitude to language. The Scots tongue became not only unfashionable but inferior to the ears of many Scots, and our political institutions, particularly the educational one, adopted and encouraged the use of English. It got to the stage where the Scots, if you like, *felt* in Scots but *thought* in a "foreign" language. That split or schism in our personality pervaded our literature. The "intellectuals", the "literati", the "educated", expected English and disapproved of anyone who wrote in Scots.

Many poets suffered this disapproval, not the least of whom was Robert Burns. He was born in 1759 and died in 1796, so he belongs to the eighteenth century, which makes this chapter out of chronological order. But although he belongs to the 18th century, he is not of it: he isn't another Pope or Dryden. Nor is he a romantic, yet in many ways his concern is partly the concern of the romantics. He is 18th century in that he writes about social institutions, religion and social manners, yet he anticipates the 19th century in that he writes about these things not in a cool, dispassionate, intellectual way, but in terms of feeling and human emotion. His poetry is full of comic quality, sympathy, warmth, generosity and vigour. He rejoices in creative energy and detests anything that devalues human worth.

He is, then, an odd mixture: akin to the eighteenth century in that his poetry deals with human nature and not with landscape or his own personal feelings, but, nevertheless, he writes with passion and commitment.

59

Burns hated, above all, hypocrisy and self-conceit. Much of his comic verse satirises and mocks the hypocrite, but none more so than his poem *Holy Willie's Prayer*, perhaps his most biting attack on complacency and arrogance. *Holy Willie's Prayer* is another dramatic monologue in which Holy Willie exposes himself to the reader for what he is: the supreme irony is that he never realises what he is or what he is doing. The poem is also an attack on Calvinism, which had shaped the views of John Knox and Scottish Presbyterianism. The Calvinists believed in predestination — that anyone's salvation depended on having been chosen or elected and not on how he/she behaved. Thus one of the chosen or elected few could really behave quite immorally, since the very fact he/she had been "chosen" guaranteed his/her salvation. Willie is in no doubt that he is one of the chosen few and, in fact, his praises of a God that has created such a manifestly unfair system are a total condemnation of Calvinism and, of course, of Willie himself.

But first read the poem. It helps if you can read it aloud in a wheedling, screeching voice which is at the same time full of complacent self-congratulation and self-satisfied arrogance. Yes, I know, it isn't easy. If you can do it, you're heading for more than your Higher English, even if it is Revised!

HOLY WILLIE'S PRAYER

O THOU, wha in the Heavens dost dwell,
Wha, as it pleases best thysel',
Sends ane to heaven and ten to hell,
   A' for thy glory,
And no for ony guid or ill
    They've done afore thee!

I bless and praise thy matchless might,
Whan thousands thou hast left in night,
That I am here afore thy sight,
   For gifts an' grace   10
A burnin' an' a shinin' light,
    To a' this place.

What was I, or my generation,
That I should get sic exaltation?
I, wha deserve most just damnation,
          For broken laws,
Sax thousand years 'fore my creation,
             Thro' Adam's cause.

When frae my mither's womb I fell,
Thou might hae plungèd me in hell,   20
To gnash my gums, to weep and wail,
          In burnin' lakes,
Where damnèd devils roar and yell,
             Chain'd to their stakes;

Yet I am here a chosen sample,
To show thy grace is great and ample;
I'm here a pillar in thy temple,
          Strong as a rock,
A guide, a buckler, an example
             To a' thy flock.   30

O Lord, thou kens what zeal I bear,
When drinkers drink, and swearers swear,
And singin' there and dancin' here,
          Wi' great an' sma':
For I am keepit by thy fear
             Free frae them a'.

But yet, O Lord! confess I must
At times I'm fash'd wi' fleshy lust;
An' sometimes too, in warldly trust,
          Vile self gets in;   40
But thou remembers we are dust,
             Defil'd in sin.

O Lord! yestreen, thou kens, wi' Meg —
Thy pardon I sincerely beg;
O! may't ne'er be a livin' plague
          To my dishonour,
An' I'll ne'er lift a lawless leg
             Again upon her.

Besides I farther maun allow,
Wi' Lizzie's lass, three times I trow —
But, Lord, that Friday I was fou,
    When I cam near her,
Or else thou kens thy servant true
    Wad never steer her.

May be thou lets this fleshly thorn
Beset they servant e'en and morn
Lest he owre high and proud should turn,
    That he's sae gifted;
If sae, they hand maun e'en be borne,
    Until thou lift it.   60

Lord, bless thy chosen in this place,
For here thou hast a chosen race;
But God confound their stubborn face,
    And blast their name,
Wha bring thy elders to disgrace
    An' public shame.

Lord, mind Gawn Hamilton's deserts,
He drinks, an' swears, an' plays at cartes,
Yet has sae mony takin' arts
    Wi' grit an' sma',   70
Frae God's ain priest the people's hearts
    He steals awa'.

An' when we chasten'd him therefor,
Thou kens how he bred sic a splore
As set the warld in a roar
    O' laughin' at us;
Curse thou his basket and his store,
    Kail and potatoes.

Lord, hear my earnest cry an' pray'r,
Against that presbyt'ry o' Ayr;   80
Thy strong right hand, Lord, make it bare
    Upo' their heads;
Lord, weigh it down, and dinna spare,
    For their misdeeds.

62

O Lord my God, that glib-tongu'd Aiken,
My very heart and soul are quakin',
To think how we stood sweatin', shakin',
            An' piss'd wi' dread,
While he, wi' hingin' lips and snakin',
            Held up his head.   90

Lord, in the day of vengeance try him;
Lord, visit them wha did employ him,
And pass not in thy mercy by them,
            Nor hear their pray'r:
But, for thy people's sake, destroy them,
            And dinna spare.

But, Lord, remember me and mine
Wi' mercies temp'ral and divine,
That I for gear and grace may shine
            Excell'd by nane,   100
And a' the glory shall be thine,
            Amen, Amen!

You see what I mean about being among the chosen few? Read again the beginning of the poem up to line 30 and you'll appreciate Willie's incredible arrogance and pride. His sin is not his responsibility —

What was I, or my generation,
That I should get sic exaltation?
I, wha deserve most just damnation,
            For broken laws,
Sax thousand years 'fore my creation,
            Thro' Adam's cause.

He claims he really is a "good" man, set aside from the rest: he doesn't drink, swear, sing or dance. Though in the next verses (lines 37 – 60) we get a more truthful picture as he describes his drinking and his licentuousness:

But yet, O Lord! confess I must
At times I'm fash'd wi' fleshly lust.

63

He, of course, isn't responsible for his "lapses"; it's God's way of ensuring he doesn't become too proud of his virtue!

> May be thou lets this fleshly thorn
> Beset they servant e'en and morn
> Lest he owre high and proud should turn,
>> That he's sae gifted;

What supreme arrogance to be so blindly proud of the fact that you're saved from pride because God thinks so highly of you. In fact, Willie is full of all the sins — pride, lust, envy, spite, vindictiveness. He is particularly envious of and spiteful towards anyone who is not part of the "chosen" few — such as Gawn Hamilton. Willie is, in the correct sense of the word, a most vicious person.

The build up in venom, vindictiveness and vengeance is really remarkable. I particularly admire the way that the penultimate verse:

> Lord, in the day of vengeance try him;
> Lord, visit them wha did employ him,
> And pass not in thy mercy by them,
>> Nor hear their pray'r:
> But, for thy people's sake, destroy them,
>> And dinna spare.

is instantly followed by:

> But, Lord, remember me and mine
> Wi' mercies temp'ral and divine,
> That I for gear and grace may shine
>> Excell'd by nane,
> And a' the glory shall be thine,
>> Amen, Amen!

thus creating an effect which is, at once, both comic and deadly serious. Willie wants and expects to get everything: wealth and material gain ('gear') on earth ('temp'ral') as well as salvation. The irony of his belief in such a God is made all the more telling by the fact that it totally escapes him.

Another dramatic monologue by Burns to which I want to draw your attention is *To a Louse* — though in this one it really is the poet himself who is speaking. The situation explains itself:

TO A LOUSE,

ON SEEING ONE ON A LADY'S BONNET AT CHURCH.

HA! wh'are ye gaun, ye crowlin' ferlie!
Your impudence protects you sairly:
I canna say but ye strunt rarely,
   Owre gauze and lace;
Tho' faith! I fear ye dine but sparely
   On sic a place.

Ye ugly, creepin', blastit wonner,
Detested, shunn'd by saunt an' sinner!
How dare ye set your fit upon her,
   Sae fine a lady?   10
Gae somewhere else, and seek your dinner
   On some poor body.

Swith, in some beggar's haffet squattle;
There ye may creep, and sprawl, and sprattle
Wi' ither kindred jumping cattle,
   In shoals and nations;
Where horn nor bane ne'er dare unsettle
   Your thick plantations.

Now haud ye there, ye're out o' sight,
Below the fatt'rels, snug an' tight;   20
Na, faith ye yet! ye'll no be right
   Till ye've got on it,
The very tapmost tow'ring height
   O' Miss's bonnet.

My sooth! right bauld ye set your nose out,
As plump and gray as onie grozet;
O for some rank mercurial rozet,
   Or fell red smeddum!
I'd gie you sic a hearty doze o't,
   Wad dress your droddum!   30

65

I wad na been surpris'd to spy
You on an auld wife's flannen toy;
Or aiblins some bit duddie boy,
                    On's wyliecoat;
But Miss's fine Lunardi! fie,
                    How daur ye do't?

O Jenny, dinna toss your head,
An' set your beauties a' abread!
Ye little ken what cursèd speed
                    The blastie's makin'!   40
Thae winks and finger-ends, I dread,
                    Are notice takin'!

O wad some Pow'r the giftie gie us
To see oursels as others see us!
It wad frae mony a blunder free us,
                    And foolish notion:
What airs in dress an' gait wad lea'e us,
                    And ev'n devotion!

Burns calls the louse impudent (line 2) and that impudence causes, initially, shock in the poet but increasingly the shock gives way to anger. But, cleverly, the focus changes from the louse to Jenny herself, who is, of course, blithely unaware of the indignity of her situation:

Ye little ken what cursed speed
                    The blastie's makin'!

But, as with much of Burns' poetry, the anecdote — told in finely observed detail — provides Burns with the opportunity to reflect on some aspect of the human condition: the louse (and all its associations with beggars and poverty) crawling on Jenny (and all her associations of lace and finery) *without her knowing it* gives rise to the reflective comment of the last stanza:

O wad some Pow'r the giftie gie us
To see oursels as others see us
It wad frae mony a blunder free us,
                    And foolish notion

With which thought, we can begin to turn our minds to the twentieth century.

– IX –

NINETEENTH AND TWENTIETH CENTURIES

Again, it has to be pointed out that in studying the history of literature the chronological measurement we call "centuries" has only limited use. At the end of Chapter VII we looked at Tennyson, who died in 1892. Tennyson we think of as the last of the romantics. Yet Robert Browning, who died before Tennyson, in many ways points forward to the new century. That is, of course, an oversimplification: much of Browning is of his age. But some of his ideas, particularly of the form of poetry, had a considerable influence on twentieth century writers. In many ways, he "feels" more modern than Keats or Byron or Shelley, even although he greatly admired those poets.

I have mentioned on several occasions now the dramatic monologue. Browning experimented with this form of poetry and contributed immensely to it. One of the most famous examples of his dramatic monologues is *My Last Duchess*. Observe the extent to which the speaker is condemned out of his own mouth.

MY LAST DUCHESS

FERRARA

> That's my last Duchess painted on the wall,
> Looking as if she were alive; I call
> That piece a wonder, now: Frá Pandolf's hands
> Worked busily a day, and there she stands.
> Will't please you sit and look at her? I said
> 'Frá Pandolf' by design, for never read
> Strangers like you that pictured countenance,
> The depth and passion of its earnest glance,
> But to myself they turned (since none puts by
> The curtain I have drawn for you, but I)
> And seemed as they would ask me, if they durst,
> How such a glance came there; so, not the first

Are you to turn and ask thus. Sir, 'twas not
Her husband's presence only, called that spot
Of joy into the Duchess' cheek: perhaps
Frá Pandolf chanced to say 'Her mantle laps
Over my Lady's wrist too much', or 'Paint
Must never hope to reproduce the faint
Half-flush that dies along her throat'; such stuff
Was courtesy, she thought, and cause enough
For calling up that spot of joy. She had
A heart . . . how shall I say? . . . too soon made glad,
Too easily impressed; she liked whate'er
She looked on, and her looks went everywhere.
Sir, 'twas all one! My favour at her breast,
The dropping of the daylight in the West,
The bough of cherries some officious fool
Broke in the orchard for her, the white mule
She rode with round the terrace — all and each
Would draw from her alike the approving speech,
Or blush, at least. She thanked men — good; but thanked
Somehow . . . I know not how . . . as if she ranked
My gift of a nine-hundred-years-old name
With anybody's gift. Who'd stoop to blame
This sort of trifling? Even had you skill
In speech — (which I have not) — to make your will
Quite clear to such an one, and say 'Just this
Or that in you disgusts me; here you miss,
Or there exceed the mark' — and if she let
Herself be lessoned so, nor plainly set
Her wits to yours, forsooth, and made excuse,
— E'en then would be some stooping, and I chuse
Never to stoop. Oh, Sir, she smiled, no doubt,
Whene'er I passed her; but who passed without
Much the same smile? This grew; I gave commands;
Then all smiles stopped together. There she stands
As if alive. Will't please you rise? We'll meet
The company below, then. I repeat,
The Count your Master's known munificence
Is ample warrant that no just pretence
Of mine for dowry will be disallowed;
Though his fair daughter's self, as I avowed

> At starting, is my object. Nay, we'll go
> Together down, Sir! Notice Neptune, though,
> Taming a sea-horse, thought a rarity,
> Which Claus of Innsbruck cast in bronze for me.

The person speaking in this poem is clearly the Duke himself. He is speaking to an envoy (a messenger) from a Count whose daughter he is about to marry. However, it is about his previous wife, his last duchess, he is speaking and as he speaks he gives away unwittingly all kinds of unpleasant aspects of his character. Clearly, he is referring to a portrait of his last Duchess, who looks in the painting "as if she were alive". The painting is normally covered by a curtain, and no-one is allowed to draw the curtain but the Duke himself. The portrait shows the Duchess in a happy mood, but that happy look was caused by any chance remark made to her: on this occasion

>   . . . perhaps
> Frá Pandolph chanced to say 'Her mantle laps
> Over my Lady's wrist too much', or 'Paint
> Must never hope to reproduce the faint
> Half-flush that dies along her throat';

and a such a remark was 'cause enough /For calling up that spot of joy'. That was because

>   . . . She had
> A heart . . . how shall I say? . . . too soon made glad,
> Too easily impressed.

And that didn't please the Duke. This woman didn't distinguish between expensive gifts and a simple offering of fruit by a silly servant. She was not sufficiently awed by his 'nine-hundred-years-old name', but he would not stoop to reprimand her. She smiled not only at him, the Duke himself, but at anyone. He got so annoyed he "gave commands"

> Then all smiles stopped together.

Did he have her killed? Anyway, clearly his sole interest is in possessions and money — as you can tell by the ending.

What else does he give away about himself? What else can you infer from what the poet says? Why does he draw the envoy's attention to the statue of Neptune as they return downstairs? Perhaps you need to check the meaning of "munificence" and "dowry" in order fully to understand the man's obsession. What of his last duchess, his wife herself? What kind of impression do you get of her? Why does the duke not share your impression? What does that say about him?

My Last Duchess is an outstanding example of the dramatic monologue and it has been an influence on twentieth century poets. I think you will agree that in style and technique it belongs more to the twentieth century than the nineteenth, even if the subject matter superficially appears dated. What it says about men's attitudes to women could hardly however, be more relevant.

The poetry of the twentieth century is rich, varied, abundant and, above all, probably familiar. Many students nowadays think only in terms of the twentieth century and forget or don't know about the several hundred years that have gone before. Most school pupils' introduction to poetry is probably the poetry of the First World War, of Wilfred Owen in particular; at any rate, most sixteen year olds will have read *Dulce et Decorum Est*. I still argue that there is no better introduction to poetry than a close look at that poem. Well read, it can have a very striking emotional impact on young people and can let them appreciate just how powerful poetry can be. It is a very persuasive poem, and is a superb example of how a skilled poet can create irony and bitterness.

But there are many many other poets worthy of your attention: Hopkins, Yeats, Eliot, Lawrence, Muir, Auden, Thomas, Larkin, Hughes, Plath — on many of whose poems I have commented in *The Practical Guide to Higher Literature* (published by Robert Gibson & Sons, 1988).

The development of literature is as patchily varied as any other development: there are experiments, some of which are excitingly successful, followed by a period of consolidation with little innovation; then a reaction by a younger generation to what is seen as dull and too conventional sets in, a flurry of experiment, excitement, and the whole process begins again. That is a gross oversimplification but you get the drift. The eighteenth century experiment with classicism eventually led to dry, arid poetry interesting only to a handful of intellectuals; a reaction set in, Wordsworth and company chose to write poetry in everyday language about landscape, nature and feelings. The early twentieth century poets prided themselves in their reaction to the soppier and more extravagant indulgences of the later romantics. Maybe that has been the case, maybe not: only time will tell.

You see there is a problem when it comes to making a critical evaluation of the work of twentieth century artists, and in this it matters not a whit whether we are dealing with poets or novelists or dramatists or painters or television scriptwriters. Judgements about art are subjective: there is no objective test of quality, no set of grade related criteria we can apply to poems, plays or paintings. The only one test there is of the value of an artwork is the test of time — if it lasts, it must be good. It really doesn't matter if you don't like *Macbeth* or *Wuthering Heights* or *Paradise Lost* or *The Mona Lisa*: they have all survived, therefore they must have something to say to us as we blunder fearfully to the twentyfirst century. It may not be quite what they had to say to the generation which conceived them, but they are still relevant. Most probably that's because they all comment on the human condition, and whatever else may have changed, human nature hasn't altered much in the last two thousand years — society may have progressed (or not), its values may have improved (or not), but people, individuals, still fall in love (and out of it), still display jealousy, envy, ambition, pride, affection, care, still fear death. But works of art which are close to us are difficult to sort out — it's difficult to know if what they say is a comment on the society and its values or whether their "message" or "theme" is an exploration of the very human condition that has created that society. If it's the latter, it will continue to nourish human beings as long as there are any. Thus, I can be fairly certain that in the year 2390 young people will still be struggling with the themes of *Hamlet*, but I am less certain that they will still be enjoying *Death of a Salesman*. Unfortunately, we won't be around to find out.

So with the poets of this century. I know those whom I admire and enjoy, but I can't say with any real conviction that they are great poets.

I have drawn your attention to verse structure, rhythm and rhyme, all of which form the "framework" of a poem. Many poems, particularly before the

71

twentieth century, had a regular verse structure, a regular rhythm and a regular rhyme scheme, the latter sometimes quite complex. Twentieth century poets began experimenting with these forms, occasionally abandoning them altogether. "Free verse" was adopted where there was neither verse structure nor rhyme. D.H. Lawrence wrote in free verse — see *Practical Guide to Literature* pages 52 – 54 for a comment on *Bat*, which is in this style. By the 1950s a reaction set in to what was regarded as excessive indulgence in formlessness. A group of poets known as "The Movement" wanted to re-establish form, to re-establish an intellectual toughness to poetry and to re-create a sense of detachment. The most notable and influential of the Movement poets is Philip Larkin, whose stance as a poet is seen by those who admire him as that of the cool, detached, intellectual observer, and by those who can't stand him as that of the jaundiced cynic. Whatever else, he did re-establish the ground rules of poetry and re-invented, so to speak, the regular verse.

One of his poems, and one of my favourites, is *Vers de Société*. The situation is simple enough: the poet has been invited to some social gathering — a cocktail party? — and the poem displays a clever shift from the poet's initial rejection of the invitation to a final acceptance. Read it carefully:

VERS DE SOCIÉTÉ

My wife and I have asked a crowd of craps
To come and waste their time and ours: perhaps
You'd care to join us? In a pig's arse, friend.
Day comes to an end.
The gas fire breathes, the trees are darkly swayed.
As so *Dear Warlock-Williams: I'm afraid* —

Funny how hard it is to be alone.
I could spend half my evenings, if I wanted,
Holding a glass of washing sherry, canted
Over to catch the drivel of some bitch
Who's read nothing but *Which*;
Just think of all the spare time that has flown

Straight into nothingness by being filled
With forks and faces, rather than repaid
Under a lamp, hearing the noise of wind,

And looking out to see the moon thinned
To an air-sharpened blade.
A life, and yet how sternly it's instilled

All solitude is selfish. No one now
Believes the hermit with his gown and dish
Talking to God (who's gone too); the big wish
Is to have people nice to you, which means
Doing it back somehow.
Virtue is social. Are, then, these routines

Playing at goodness, like going to church?
Something that bores us, something we don't do well
(Asking that ass about his fool research)
But try to feel, because, however crudely,
It shows us what should be?
Too subtle, that. Too decent, too. Oh hell,

Only the young can be alone freely.
The time is shorter now for company,
And sitting by a lamp more often brings
Not peace, but other things.
Beyond the light stand failure and remorse
Whispering *Dear Warlock-Williams: Why, of course* —

LARKIN

The invitation, somewhat self-mockingly expressed, is in italics at the beginning. The poet's reaction to it couldn't be couched in language any more direct and forthright. The poet's reply is *"Dear Warlock-Williams: I'm afraid* —": we expect him to decline the invite. But then Larkin begins to balance loneliness against banal, empty, tedious social chatter, becoming in the process gradually more philosophical about our need to be involved with each other, until finally, driven by his fears of loneliness and failure, he accepts. But what I want you to examine carefully are the techniques of verse structure and rhyme scheme. Look again at verse one.

My wife and I have asked a crowd of craps
To come and waste their time and ours: perhaps
You'd care to join us? In a pig's arse, friend.
Day comes to an end.
The gas fire breathes, the trees are darkly swayed.
And so *Dear Warlock-Williams: I'm afraid* —

73

What is the rhyme scheme? — *a a b b c c* : very regular and quite simple. What about verse two? — *a b b c c a* . Verse three — *a b c c b a* . Verse four — *a b b c a c* . Verse five — *a b a c c b* . And verse six — *a a b b c c* — back to the regular simple scheme of the first verse. In other words the scheme gets increasingly complex in keeping with the increasing complexity of his ideas. But look how he alters rhythm to create effect. Remember what I have said about *iambic pentameter*?

⌣ ╱ ⌣ ╱⌣ ╱ ⌣╱ ⌣╱
My wife and I have asked a crowd of craps
⌣ ╱ ⌣ ╱ ⌣╱ ⌣ ╱ ⌣ ╱
To come and waste their time and ours: perhaps

But that rhythm is broken by the sense in the next line:

You'd care to join us? In a pig's arse, friend.

The rhythm fits, but if you read the line as iambic pentameter, the sense breaks down. He deliberately uses enjambement at the end of line two —

　　　　　　　　. . . . : perhaps
You'd care to join us?

and then creates a break before the reply. That technique draws attention to the reply and helps, along with word-choice, to make it shocking. The rhythm of iambic pentameter is picked up again in the final line of the verse.

I could go on, but I shan't. The rest is up to you. But look carefully at the rhythm of each verse, and then of the final verse: what do you notice? Some of the images are very haunting.

　　　　And looking out to see the moon thinned
　　　　To an air-sharpened blade.

and

　　　　And sitting by a lamp more often brings
　　　　Not peace, but other things.
　　　　Beyond the light stand failure and remorse

Larkin often begins by using a concrete experience and moves out and beyond it to the abstract. This poem is really no exception. But it is tightly written to a complex set of rules, though finally and ironically it explores a fineness of feeling to which many of the more excessive romantics couldn't begin to aspire.

– X –

CONCLUSION

We are coming to an end of this very rapid guided-tour through the history of poetry and of the ideas — at least some of them — reflected in or even created by that poetry. I know that for many people poetry is an abusive six letter word, a turn-off, the antithesis of enjoyment or good fun. If that is still how you feel, then this book has not succeeded in one of its aims; yet if you have read this far, then maybe poetry is that little bit less boring than it at first seemed. If people are turned off by poetry, it's because of how they have been taught: of course poetry is difficult and demanding, but it's also rewarding. Poetry deals with our experience and our language, and none of us can escape either.

I said way back on page 41 that I would discuss *metaphor* and now is a fitting time to discuss it, for the very concept of metaphor illustrates what I mean by the nature of poetry. Some people would claim that a metaphor is simply a figure of speech, just as alliteration, personification, oxymoron are figures of speech. I was taught at school that a *simile* had a *like* or an *as* in it, whereas a metaphor hadn't. Thus

>   Kevin was like a lion in the fight

is a simile, whereas

>   Kevin was a lion in the fight

is a metaphor. But my teacher told us that a long time ago, and I have since learned that much of what I was taught at school was not only irrelevant, it was wrong. That definition of metaphor is as superficial as it is useless. Metaphor is not a device, a figure of speech, it is the basis of literature. Now I know that this is a concept which is not easy to grasp, but there is a sense in which every story is a metaphor — every story has an implied meaning and is its own comment on human existence. Put another way, every story — and I am using "story" in its widest sense to include drama, the novel and poetry — is both particular and universal: the story is about itself, but it also makes a comment which has universal application. And it is that universal application which contains its truth. For example, the story of Christ, whether or not you accept it as historical fact, is nevertheless metaphorically true: Christ was too revolutionary in his teachings, especially about love and the nature of forgiveness, for human beings to tolerate him, and so he was executed. If you remember what happened, or what was supposed to have happened, the people were given a choice: should Barabbus, the thief, be saved from execution or should it be Christ, the revolutionary teacher — and the people chose to save a common criminal from the cross, since thieves are easier to live with than someone who teaches the forgiveness of enemies. Thieves are less dangerous. That story may or may not have taken place, but really that doesn't matter, since it is what the story says about human beings that is true: what it says about love, forgiveness and human nature is as true today as it was two thousand years ago.

All the poems in this book are metaphors in that sense: they all say something about human beings and about the human condition. Whenever you write, say a story for your Review of Personal Studies, you are creating a metaphor: your story will make some kind of comment. If you can grasp what I am saying about metaphor, you are well on your way to understanding how poetry, literature and art work.

There is just a bit more to add — and it's this bit that makes literature so important to me. An author creates the metaphor, invents the story using language and his powerful imagination, drawing on his awareness of his experience of life. All that is true, but what really matters is the significance the story takes on when you, the reader, read it. You then draw on your knowledge of language, your imagination and your awareness of experience to re-create the metaphor. And, of course, the more you read, the more developed your language and imagination will become, and the more aware you will be of your own experience. But the essential point is that the story has no significance on its own, it doesn't even exist, till you read it and relate it to yourself.

None of my English teachers at school was particularly inspiring: they taught *Hamlet* and *The Canterbury Tales* as though these were geometric theorems. As long as you knew your notes, painstakingly dictated, and the odd quotation, that was all that mattered. All literature was a museum piece, set in time, about as interesting and relevant as a monolithic tomb. That *The Pardoner's Tale* was written for a "modern" audience who might have enjoyed what they read was a thought as alien and remote as the idea that Pythagoras' squared hypotenuse might have blown the minds of a few of his Greek friends. There was never any question of enjoying a poem (or a play or a pre-twentieth century novel) and even less of being involved in what it had to say. But yet, when you stop to think about it, Chaucer's contemporaries must have enjoyed his tales, and certainly they must have been involved in what the tales had to say. It is precisely what they had to say, and still have to say, that has made them last. People read *The Canterbury Tales* or *My Last Duchess* or *Vers de Société* not because they have to in order to pass Higher English, but because these poems say something 'to them'. *The Pardoner's Tale* says something about greed and the fact that human beings will corrupt their souls to acquire material possessions — and that is as true today as it was in the fourteenth century. Poems do not belong in museums; however "old" they are, they say something about that world out there, something significant, which makes that world that bit easier to understand.

This lesson is perhaps the hardest of all to grasp. I can guarantee that throughout the 1990s candidates, in whatever literature exam they are sitting, will insist on regurgitating their learned-up notes, clinging on to what someone else has said about the poem, like some novice in the pool afraid to let go of the side, afraid to enjoy the sensation of being alive in the water. Put the notes to the side, and become aware of the effect the poem is having on you.

What matters is what *you* get out of the poem, what the poem means to *you*. That doesn't mean, of course, that you have *carte blanche* to say whatever you like. You can't just use the poem as a pad from which to launch your own views on whatever you think the subject matter might be. You have to work at the poem, teasing out the meaning. You might well then ask how to go about doing just that, and there is no easy answer. T.S. Eliot, one of the major poets and critics of this century, said that there is no method except to be very intelligent. You might not be disposed to finding that remark particularly helpful, and so, as an aid to your intelligence, let me remind you of the method I find useful: the three questions —

(a)   What is the poem about?

(b)   What are its effects on me?

(c)   How have these effects been achieved?

Answer *(a)* in terms of themes: is it about greed or jealousy or regret or unrequited love or about how things change or (more likely) about how things don't change? When it comes to answering *(b)* think of how you have reacted: have I found the poem sad, funny, enlightening, boring . . . have I enjoyed the beauty of its language, the cleverness of its wit, the accuracy of its sentiments? When it comes to *(c)*, the real business of practical criticism, think of all the devices that have been discussed in this book. Of the devices or techniques used by poets, the one most often neglected by critics is the use of *sound*. Remind yourself about what I said right at the beginning of the book about the importance of sound: rhythm and rhyme-scheme contribute to the overall effect of sound, but don't forget all the other techniques to do with sound, such as the kind of consonants, the length of the vowels, alliteration.

Poets also use images to create effects. An image, as I've said before, is difficult to define, though the best working definition is to think of images as word pictures. The trouble is the very word "picture" connotes or suggests something visual, something that can be seen, whereas some images appeal to our senses of touch, smell, taste and hearing as well as sight. It is easier to examine how an image works and whether or not it is appropriate. Edwin Morgan, a Glasgow-born poet of considerable distinction, has written a number of sonnets, one of which begins:

> A mean wind wanders through the backcourt trash.
> Hackles on puddles rise . . .

"Hackles on puddles rise" is an image. What is it an image of? Always examine the language used: "Hackles" — what has hackles? A dog? A cat? You think a dog . . . Why is the image of a dog appropriate, given the first line? And why do its hackles rise? Or rather why do the "hackles" on puddles rise? Once you identify the image, it becomes easier to say why it is appropriate. Given that the poem is about the back court of a dilapidated Glasgow tenement "condemned to stand", the image of the dog becomes very appropriate.

You have also to bear in mind the structure of the verse the poet has chosen to use: *rhyming verse* — in which case you should work out the rhyme scheme to determine its contribution to sound and meaning; *blank verse* — where there is no rhyme, but there is a regular rhythm which contributes to sound and meaning: and *free verse* — where there is neither rhyme nor regular rhythm, the absence of both of which contributes to sound and meaning. Does the sentence structure fit the line and verse structure, or are there run-on lines and run-on verses? Sentence structure which does not quite fit verse structure often creates a subtle tension in the poem. You also need to note word-choice and allow the connotations of words to play in your imagination, working out the ways in which the connotations are appropriate to the effect created.

But you must never lose sight of the fact that an awareness of these technical devices is not an end in itself; what matters is your engagement with the poem and your involvement in what it says to you in this the last decade of the twentieth century. We are all products of our time and our culture: we are the product of over a thousand years of the events, the thoughts, the aspirations, the disappointments, the intrigues that have taken place on this little island. But our culture of which we are an indisputable part is, in many ways, alien to us because we are so unaware of it. This book is intended to make you that little bit more aware. It is intended to give you some kind of perspective, to let you know where poems "fit" in the history of ideas. The more you become aware of our past, the more you will be able to make sense of the present, and the more sense you have of the present, the more you will realise that what happened in the past is not dead and fossilised but is an organic part of what we have become. Poetry is a vital part of that process because the poet not only reflects that history, he helps create it. Maybe one day you'll add to it yourself.

If this book has aroused your curiosity, then I shall be well pleased.

ACKNOWLEDGEMENTS

The publisher is grateful to the following for permission to use copyright material in this book.

Vers de Société from *HIGH WINDOWS*

by Philip Larkin

Reprinted by permission of the publisher Faber and Faber, Limited.